Alexis C. Bell

A framework for

Extraordinary Relationships

Without guilt, shame or fear

By

Alexis C. Bell

A Framework for Extraordinary Relationships Without Guilt, Shame or Fear

Copyright © April 2013 by
Alexis C. Bell
All Rights Reserved

This publication, in whole or in part, may not be reproduced, stored in a retrieval system or transmitted in any form by any means be it electronic, mechanical, photocopy, recording, scanning or otherwise, except as permitted under Section 107 or 108 of the 1976 United States Copyright Act, without prior written permission of the Author.

ISBN-13: 978-1484827307

ISBN-10: 1484827309

Charlotte, North Carolina
United States of America

Table of Contents

Forward 7

Acknowledgements 10

   Permissions 14

Dedication 16

Part I: Setting Up the Framework 17

   Introduction 17

   Universal Truths 20

      My Relationship to Universal Truths 21

   Choice 23

   Crucial Conversations 26

      Core Values 26

      Prioritization 27

      First Domino 28

      Safe Space 29

Part II: Relating to Each Other 30

   Connecting 31

      Physical Connection 31

      Intellectual Connection 31

      Emotional Connection 32

      Spiritual Connection 33

   Love Languages 34

      Words of Affirmation 34

      Quality Time 36

      Receiving Gifts 36

      Acts of Service 37

      Physical Touch 38

What's My Love Language? 38
Information Processing 39
    Input versus Output 44
Conversation Timing 45
    A Lesson in Interrupting 50
    Default Flow Style 52
Myers-Briggs® 54
    Temperament Types 57
    Personality Types 57
    What's My Personality Type? 58
Anger 59
    Self-Pity 59
    Toilet Seat Trigger 60
Lizard Brain 62
    Sex & Gender Differences 63
    Sabotage 64
Perseverance 67

Part III: Using the Framework 71
Who Do You Have To Be? 71
    Compassionate 71
    Courageous 72
    Vulnerable 72
    Empowered 73
    Accountable 73
    Authentic 73
    Present 74
The Upset 75
Periodic Check-In 77

- *It's Time* 77
- *Celebrate Successes* 78
- *To Connect* 78
- *Under Stress* 79
- *Feelings* 81
  - *Non-Feeling Warning Signs* 83
- *Needs* 85
- *Mirror* 89
  - *You Don't Appreciate Me* 89
  - *You Don't Take Care of Me Financially* 92
- *Children* 98
  - *Initial Dating* 98
  - *Pre-Meeting* 98
  - *Initial Meeting* 99
  - *During the Relationship* 99
- *Stages* 102
  - *Initiation Stage* 102
  - *Free Flow Stage* 104
  - *Clarity Stage* 106
  - *Resolution Stage* 115
- *Requests* 118
  - *Determine What You Want* 118
  - *Leave the Judgments Behind* 120
  - *Attachment to an Outcome* 121
  - *Bring a Solution* 123
  - *Ask for What You Need* 126
- *Wellbeing* 130
- *Outside Influences* 131

Disagreement Postmortem 133
Evolution 134
    Life Lessons 135
Part IV: Exercises 137
    Appreciation 139
        The Love Letter 139
        Favorites 139
    Perception Pie Chart 140
        Sample of an Exaggeration 145
        Interpretation 146
    Positive Perspective 150
    Judge-Your-Neighbor Worksheet 154
        Sample Judge-Your-Neighbor Worksheet Completed 165
    Nonviolent Communication Model 169
        Sample NVC Model Worksheet Completed 170
    When I Say... 172
    60-Day Fear Challenge 173
About the Author 174
References 175

Appendix A – Myers-Briggs® Personality Types 179
Appendix B – Sex & Gender Differences in the Brain 183
Appendix C – Feelings when your needs are NOT satisfied 188
Appendix D – Feelings when your needs ARE satisfied 190
Appendix E – Evaluations Masquerading As Feelings 192
Appendix F – Matrix of Needs and Satisfiers 199
Appendix G – Needs Inventory 203

Forward

Relationships are one of the more complex and difficult aspects of being human. We seek the acceptance and love that truly completes the connection to love and to be loved. As we move through our lives with our family, partner, spouse, work, friends, and social situations, we seek safe relationships. This is easier said than done! Yet we plod on. Although some of us have the tools we need there is no guarantee, that we can successfully navigate the paradigms in our relationships.

There is only love and fear – we act from a place of love or a place of fear. We seek to operate in the love mode, but the lines between love and fear can be blurred. Love allows us to create the relationships we need, fear impedes us in a multitude of ways. Anger is the most common result of fear. Acknowledging and knowing the place you are in is a vital component to building and maintaining a healthy, functional relationship.

One of the keys to having a successful relationship is strong, active communication. We can talk to each other, but are we truly conveying and understanding the context of the conversation? Are we more intent on expressing our thoughts instead of truly listening to what the other person is saying? How can we improve our ability to talk to each other and establish practices that empower us to convey our message? Some Native Americans have a method of communication, which consists of the speaker holding a stone. This effectively honors the speaker and creates a respectful atmosphere for the listener. That is the first step to building a strong relationship.

Throughout this book Alexis provides insight, stories, examples, and exercises to strengthen our relationships. She focuses more on the most intimate and coveted relationship of all, that of partner or spouse. Yet many of the processes can be used in other relationships as well. Keeping true to her admitted geekish nature, she lays out a methodical approach to working on our relationships in ways that we often overlook, forget, or simply do not know. Take in her stories. They share real world examples of how a variety of people built powerful, working relationships.

Open yourself to the journey Alexis gives to you, and receive these gifts written with love.

~ Debra Sloan
- *Aunt of Alexis and her biggest advocate*
- *North Carolina Department of Agriculture and Consumer Services, Agriculture Economic Developer and Aquaculture Specialist*
- *Lives in an incredible spot in the Appalachian Mountains*

> One of the first things I teach my students in Pathology class is that the human body will always try to balance itself when under attack from pathogens. Balance may not lead to restoration or even normal function, but the human organism will attempt to reach for whatever state of equilibrium it can obtain. With time and sometimes outside assistance, we can find a new balance. This book is the medicine we need to reach our optimal life balance because relationships are a core factor in our overall wellness.
>
> ~ James Willer, PhD.

Acknowledgements

To all of you mentioned below: *Know that you made a difference.*

Heartfelt appreciation goes to **LeeAnna Waldrop** for the countless hours spent editing this book. Many authors carry great emotional attachment to each written word. Thoughtful consideration is given to every aspect of the message we attempt to convey. It is not an easy task to hand over our work for critique. However, each modification was suggested by LeeAnna in a kind and careful way that showed great respect for the creative process. It was a sincere pleasure to work with her.

Without a strong foundation, you cannot even begin to build the structure required for you to be your best self. There are a few people that greatly contributed to my foundation which will always live in a special place in my heart.

- **Honey**: for being a strong woman and a loving great-grandmother. *(In loving memory)*
- **Grandma Annie**: for sacrificing her retirement to raise one more generation and for the gift of tolerance.
- **Da-Dad**: for the gift of the unreasonable request and for loving me enough to make that last phone call to me. *(In loving memory)*
- **Mom**: for the gift of individuality and teaching me independence.
- **Dad**: for the hours of conversations that expanded my mind and most especially for celebrating my successes with me.
- **My brother & sisters**: for inspiring me to go beyond my self-imposed limits and for allowing me to be me (faults and all). *(In loving memory of Landis)*
- **Aunt Debra**: for the gift of what it means to be a great daughter and for being a constant inside the swirl of chaos.

- **Aunt Polly**: for the gift of laughter and teaching me it's never too late to make a significant change in your life.
- **Uncle Larry & Uncle Pete**: for the gift of living your passion; to identify what you love and figure out how to get someone to pay you for it.
- **Doug Ward**: for exemplifying the impact an exceptional teacher can have on one of his students and for believing in me even when I wasn't sure I could believe in myself. *(In loving memory)*
- **Dale Fountain**: for being my longest and dearest friend and for knowing all of my stories and sticking around anyway.
- **Robert Venables**: for the gift of dedication to a cause bigger than yourself and for the two years of Friday night dinners and meaningful conversation on campus.
- **Andy Barbee & Erik Lioy**: for being my champions in the early years.
- **James Willer**: for being our tribal elder in all things that really mattered and for being a role model author who suggested to publish this book now instead of waiting for the unattainable state of perfection.
- **Claudie and Rene Strickland**: for the gift of generosity and for being angels that walk this earth.
- **Past Relationships**: for walking the path with me during this journey of self-exploration.

This painting represents the gifts that the Creator gives in his expression of love. This is seen in many ways during the transformation process of personal growth. The butterfly becomes a beacon for that metamorphosis as it dances in the spirit of our hearts.

~ Christopher J. Rowland

"Gifts" (70"x40" oil on canvas).
Painted in 1991 © Christopher J Rowland

Permissions

The following artists, authors and publishers graciously granted permission to include their previously published work in this book. It is with great appreciation that I acknowledge their contribution to my life during my exploration and thus wanted to share their impactful lessons with you, the readers.

Gifts

"Gifts" painting (70"x40" oil on canvas). Copyright 1991 by Christopher J. Rowland. The painting was reprinted with written permission provided by the artist and the explanation was written by the artist exclusively for this book.

Myers Briggs ®

Myers-Briggs®, Myers-Briggs Type Indicator®, MBTI®, and Personality Differences Questionnaire® are all registered trademarks with CPP, Inc.

Modified and reproduced by special permission of the Publisher, CPP, Inc. Mountain View, CA 94043 from Introduction to Type, Sixth Edition by Isabel Briggs Myers. Copyright 1998 by Peter B. Myers and Katharine D. Myers. All rights reserved. Further reproduction is prohibited without the Publisher's written consent.

Love Languages

The 5 Love Languages: The Secret to Love That Lasts (Chapman, 1992/2010). The concept of love languages in this chapter was adapted with written permission from Moody Publishers.

Non-Feeling Warning Signs

The Evaluations Masquerading As Feelings list (Lasater, 2003) in this chapter and appendix was reprinted with written permission from Ike Lasater.

Life Lessons

Text from pp. 190-1 {"Our deepest fear... liberates others."} from A RETURN TO LOVE by MARIANNE WILLIAMSON. Copyright © 1992 by Marianne Williamson. Reprinted by written permission of HarperCollins Publishers.

Judge-Your-Neighbor Worksheet ©

The Judge-Your-Neighbor Worksheet© is a copyrighted excerpt from the book *I Need Your Love – Is That True?* (Katie, 2002). It was reprinted with written permission from Byron Katie International, Inc.

Needs Inventory

The concept for the appendix was adapted from the *Feelings Inventory* by Dr. Marshall B. Rosenberg with written permission from CNVC.

© 2005 by Center for Nonviolent Communication
Website: www.cnvc.org
Email: cnvc@cnvc.org
Phone: +1.505.244.4041

Dedication

This book is dedicated to my two daughters, Erika and Cheyanna. They are the reason I try so hard and why I never gave up. They are my inspiration to reach deep down and pull out my extraordinary self. *Anything worthwhile I have ever done was a direct result of my undying love for them.*

Part I: Setting Up the Framework

Introduction

> *"When you are **disconnected** from each other,*
> *everything seems to fall apart.*
> *When you are **connected** to each other,*
> *everything becomes possible."*

Relationships prior to implementing this approach to communication and overall framework for an extraordinary relationship looked very different than what I experience now. Previously, the overarching theme of the relationship was that it always started out great and fantastic, only to crash and burn in the end.

Before, disagreements were arguments that escalated over time without any kind of resolution. Both parties were left hurt and wounded with no hope in sight. The result was a slow chipping away at the relationship. This created cracks in the foundation that eventually crumbled and resulted in the relationship ending with both of us looking around wondering what had happened.

Now, disagreements inside the realm of an extraordinary relationship without guilt, shame, or fear leaves us actually feeling *closer* to each other than before the issue arose. When you are disconnected from each other, everything seems to fall apart. What was so important in one instance just doesn't even matter anymore. You wonder why you even cared about it at all. Facing losing the relationship puts priorities in perspective. On the other hand, when the two of you are connected, and I mean *really* connected with each other, then everything becomes possible. When you can live inside something truly extraordinary the relationship becomes the springboard to an exceptional life.

I noticed early on that challenges were actually opportunities for growth. The key was often to not give in to my knee jerk reaction and instead actively seek clarity. For instance, when one partner first told me that he requested a relationship with no boundaries, what I *heard* was that he sought freedom to do whatever he wanted. I heard that he didn't care enough about me to even want boundaries around what I did or didn't do; that it just didn't matter to him. I heard that he was not invested in the relationship and that he was afraid of commitment. However, as time went by it became evident that <u>none</u> of that was true.

What I realized was that he said he wanted for us to hold the space for our relationship to be one that could not be fit into a mere container. He wanted to have a relationship where we could *ask* for what we needed without the restraints of what our preconceived notions of what "relationship" was. We both acknowledged that neither of us knew exactly what that would look like and that not knowing brought up a lot of fear for the both of us. In the end though, I was finally able to understand that what he *really* meant was that he wanted me to know the relationship was so unbelievably important that no matter what events unfolded during our path together, that we would be able to make it through. I heard that what he wanted was a relationship with me that would not only stand the test of time, but that it would thrive and blossom into something so wonderful and beautiful that we could not even begin to imagine how extraordinary it was going to be.

So, how did I come to this amazing discovery you may ask? At my core, I am a scientist completely fascinated with the scientific method. Yes, it is true -- I am a *brainiac with geekish tendencies*. That being said, life as a brainiac affords me the ability to look at things in a novel way. One of my great joys is to break complex concepts down into their base parts in an effort to better understand how everything fits together. This discovery process provides clarity into how it all works. Initially I applied this method in order to create a model for relationships in my own life. However, over time it became evident that the framework could benefit others as well. The outcome was an exploration that led to a structure with reproducible results.

Keep in mind, the path can be difficult at times with tears and even tantrums until you can learn how to communicate effectively with each other. If you want an easy fix for the relationship with three little things to change in your daily routine that will suddenly make everything perfect, this is not the book for you. However, if you are willing to *stand in the fire* with your partner and make the relationship a priority, you have just taken the most important step in the health of your relationship.

This book is a testament to what is possible when you ask for what you want, when you can stretch way beyond your comfort zone, and make concentrated efforts to explore your fears as well as your dreams. It is how you can have an extraordinary relationship without guilt, shame, or fear.

Universal Truths

> *"In relating to each other this way, we have created the foundation from which significant and life changing conversations have catapulted our healing process, our evolution as individual human beings and resulted in an extraordinary relationship without guilt, shame or fear."*

There are concepts that hold true through all scenarios with only a few extreme exceptions. These threads that are weaved throughout the human experience which can be shared by us all are known as **Universal Truths**. In designing the framework for extraordinary relationships, we attempted to identify those lessons and insights that held true through all of our experiences. I wanted to pinpoint the common threads so that I could then create reproducible results.

My Relationship to Universal Truths

I was able to skip a number of classes, sometimes even a few grades, in middle and high schools when it came to math and science. At the time, it seemed like I was ahead of the curve, but during my college days while attaining my bachelor's degree, I realized that I had actually missed out because I was never exposed to subjects like geometry, statistics, calculus, or physics. Skipping those classes meant the first time I saw them was in college. Since they were completely new to me, I met each fresh concept with wonder. I was amazed at the presentation of an absolutely new perspective. It gave me entirely new ways of looking at the world.

During my last semester of undergrad, I took my very first physics class. Physics introduced to me the concept of universal truths. In my mind, I saw it like this: Think of the film *Willie Wonka & the Chocolate Factory* (Margulies & Wolper, 1971). In that movie, there was a scene with the character, Mike TV, where Mr. Wonka was explaining how the television process worked. Mr. Wonka "zapped" a Wonka-bar, the candy bar split into a billion pieces, flew overhead in what looked like a stream of static, and was reassembled into a clear picture on the television set at the other side of the room, albeit smaller, in 3-dimensions and completely edible.

To me, in the search for universal truths physics takes the realm of what is possible (the stream of static) and pulls out the details (the universal truths) that apply to everything. Gravity is an example of a universal truth. Admittedly, given certain contexts such as outer space or atomic-levels, gravity breaks down as a universal truth. However, it certainly does hold true in general terms inside the normal, everyday experience.

This is the space where universal truths hold true in the context of an extraordinary relationship. In math terms, there are always outliers; those one-offs that simply don't conform to the rest of the data. However, when examining life lessons that we can learn from and apply with reproducible results, we need to pay the most attention to the areas that will provide us with the greatest impact. Given the majority of situations in most scenarios, universal truths can provide profound insights in how to achieve a desired outcome even when we aren't absolutely sure it is even attainable.

One such universal truth answers the question, "What really matters?" During a period in my life, I became very interested in determining what was really important. I wanted to know what truly mattered. So, I spent a great deal of time listening to people that were at or near the end of their life. When faced with the end of their lives, whether it had been relatively short or exceptionally long, I asked them to share with me what was the one thing they thought I should know.

Not one person said they wished they had a bigger house, a better car, a faster boat, made more money, gotten the promotion, or spent more time at work. While the answer was not exactly surprising, the consistency of it was. They all said the same thing. Every single person said *they wished they had spent more time with the people that they loved*. When given the opportunity to look back over the course of an entire lifetime, what really mattered when it was all said and done was *meaningful relationships*. It was the key to living a fulfilled life, to maintaining inner peace, and to loving those most precious to you from a place of harmony.

While going through the process of designing the communication strategy for relationships, I have identified universal truths that have consistently held true for me and my partner within our experience. This framework has become the filter through which we communicate. In relating to each other this way, we have created the foundation from which significant and life changing conversations have catapulted our healing process, our evolution as individual human beings and resulted in an extraordinary relationship without guilt, shame or fear.

Choice

> *"Where you are in life is a direct result of decisions you have made. If you want something to change, then choose a different path."*

It all boils down to *choice*. The ability to have an extraordinary relationship begins with choosing to have one. If I look back into my life, there was one pivotal moment when this lesson came to light. When I was in my late teens, I was driven to succeed. I had learned at an early age that if I wanted something, I had to make it happen on my own. I used to say there wasn't exactly a line of people volunteering to take care of me. If it was going to happen, I had to do it myself.

That kind of self-reliance allowed me to accomplish some pretty lofty goals later in life, however during that timeframe it created a disconnect whenever I came across people who in my view were not "successful". While my definition of successful is completely different today than it was back then, it seemed to be a purely financial characterization at the time. In general, as a teenager I had a very difficult time understanding people who would do something differently than what I would do.

Part of that period of my life involved a spiritual exploration. While I was particularly closed minded in one area, I was incredibly open minded in another. I was fascinated by other people's viewpoints related to their spiritual path. I actively sought people from different backgrounds so that I could attempt to gain a better understanding of their religion. I never passed up an opportunity to listen so that I could learn about their experience. It was this thirst for knowledge that led me to meet a woman that would forever change my perspective.

My grandmother lived in the tiny Tellico community within a valley just outside a small, rural town situated in the Smokey Mountains of western North Carolina. Her cattle ranch that later became a rainbow trout farm was easily a half an hour from town where the last few miles before arriving at her house required travelling on a dusty, winding, gravel road. It was the proverbial, "Over the river and through the woods to Grandmother's house we go."

There was a woman that lived in the valley near my grandmother. If I had to take a guess, I'd say she was nearing 100 years old at the time. She was a thin little old lady with weathered, tanned skin adorned with wrinkles. She wore a long-sleeved hand sewn frontier dress, ancient work boots that may have been as old as she was, and she had her grey hair pulled back into a simple bun. She lived in a one room cabin that I imagined her husband had built for them back when they were just starting a life together. The cabin had dirt floors, no electricity, no running water, and an outhouse that was well... outside in the yard. She was rarely seen out and about with the exception of the monthly trips to town for supplies. Her truck was from the 1930s and probably had a top speed of about 20 miles per hour.

I remember having judgments about her life. I remember thinking I would be miserable if I had to live like that. I could not imagine the possibility that anyone could be even remotely happy in that kind of scenario. I distinctly remember feeling sorry for her.

Then one early spring afternoon, I had the most amazing opportunity to listen to her. In anticipation, I had a whole host of questions I wanted to ask her. I had created categories and subcategories. All of my questions were carefully arranged so as to maximize my time with her. I loved efficiency even back then. Yet none of that mattered. I did not get to ask one single predetermined question because while she was talking, she smiled and said this: "I love to wash dishes because the hot water helps my hands."

What? My brain screeched to a halt as I attempted to reconcile what she said. You *like* to wash dishes? It *helps* your hands? What kind of perspective was *that*? I detested chores. If my hands were riddled with arthritis, my teenage mind imagined that I'd be pretty angry that I even *had* to do the dishes. However, when I could take myself out of the picture and merely observe her experience, I realized she had just given me an incredibly profound gift; the gift of choice. She purposefully chose a perspective that would enhance her life rather than detract from it. She *chose* to find the good in whatever she was dealt. In listening to her further, she *chose* the feeling of being happy in everything she did. She was grateful for every aspect of her life and as a result she was living purely in the moment in a constant state of peace and wellbeing.

The woman, who I had felt sorry for earlier, said something so simple and so impactful that I instantly retracted the initial thought. Instead, I found myself feeling sad for anyone who did not adopt her line of thinking. A choice; it was a choice.

It opened up an entire world of possibilities. Over time, I came to realize that if your perspective related to happiness is a choice, then *everything* is actually a choice. I learned that, *"Where you are in life is a direct result of decisions you have made. If you want something to change, then choose a different path."* In the context of an extraordinary relationship, it all boils down to choice. Choose to have one, declare it with conviction, and then take the steps to make it a reality.

Crucial Conversations

A crucial conversation is one of those pivotal conversations that alter the course of the relationship. It sets up the structure for how you will obtain what you both want within the relationship. There are four primary components involved in a successful crucial conversation for extraordinary relationships: core values, prioritization, first domino, and safe space.

Core Values

Before making the decision to move forward with the commitment of utilizing the framework, take a moment to evaluate the core values you each bring to the table. Do you consider honesty to be the most important characteristic in the world while your partner feels completely comfortable lying in any situation if it takes the immediate pressure off in the moment? Do you hold yourself to the highest standard of integrity willing to amass great personal sacrifice in order to maintain that level of integrity? Does your partner exemplify the same standard? Is it a crucial part of your core being to give to others while your partner believes taking care of their self to the exclusion of others is perfectly fine and is absolutely confused every time you want to help others? Do you share the same viewpoint on the majority of core values while only disagreeing on ones that are <u>not</u> deal breakers?

Really take inventory of yourself and your partner's core values. Understand they do not show up in terms of absolutes. It's not an "all or nothing" classification. Core values are on a gradient. In other words, consider rating each one on a scale of 1 to 10 in terms of importance where not having it "1" doesn't matter at all and "10" is an absolute deal breaker.

```
                        Integrity
   Not                                         Extremely
Important  1 – 2 – 3 – 4 – 5 – 6 – 7 – 8 – 9 - 10  Important
                                ▲
 not having it:  doesn't matter    is a deal breaker
```

Explore your core values together and see how closely they align. While it is possible to bridge that gap (if there is one), know that *core values are at the center of who you are as a person. They are the filter through which you make decisions.* If you are willing to share a life with someone, the consideration of core values is an important conversation to have.

Prioritization

The current craze is for consultants to tell their followers, "You have to make *yourself* the priority." In one aspect, I completely agree. It reminds me of the safety instructions provided by the airline steward(ess) when you fly on a plane. "In the event of cabin depressurization, the oxygen masks will deploy. If you are travelling with a small child, place the mask over your mouth first before assisting the child." This makes perfect sense. You cannot help the other person if you are passed out from a lack of oxygen. However, the piece that many consultants are failing to communicate is that if you make yourself the *only* priority, i.e. you make yourself the priority to the exclusion of everyone else then you are just being selfish. Decide if there is even room in your life for another person. Make the decision to include them or exclude them and to what extent. Communicate that to your partner.

If you decide to include the other person and move forward with the relationship, make a verbal agreement to make the relationship a priority; not *the* priority, but *a* priority. For instance, if you have children and this is a new relationship for you, the children must be take precedence over the fledgling relationship. It is important to disclose to each other where the relationship falls within the hierarchy of priorities.

Keep in mind that this is fluid. Over time, as the relationship grows the priorities can change. When the children grow up and move out of the house, the relationship can move up a notch; not that the children are less important, not at all. It is just that the amount of time invested into the children becomes less as they begin to live their own lives. Simultaneously, the relationship becomes more ingrained within your life thus requiring more of your time. *Where you place your focus is what will show up in your life.* Periodically check-in and reevaluate the status of where the relationship falls within the hierarchy of prioritization.

First Domino

Agree to hold the space for an extraordinary relationship without guilt, shame, or fear. Agree to stop whatever you are doing and have a purposeful dialogue when one of you has the need to talk. Agree to come to each other when either of you feel any emotion which bubbles up that is other than feeling calm, centered and balanced or think any thought that could impact the relationship. The key is to initiate the conversation when the first domino falls. Do not fool yourself into believing, "If I don't say anything, it will resolve itself and go away" or "It's not *that* big of a deal, I don't want to rock the boat."

The danger is that if you do not catch the issue when that very first domino falls, there may be a cascading effect that could eventually create a significant impact large enough to manifest as a full blown crises. Agree to support each other when the smallest, tiniest thing pops up. Talk it through while it's little and the emotional attachment is small. Recognize this is not putting an undue burden on the relationship. It is actually a preventative measure to keep the major crises from occurring in the first place. *Agree to have a dialogue every time that first domino falls.*

Safe Space

Agree to hold a safe space for each other. You must create a space where your partner feels safe enough to divulge their inner most thoughts and feelings. You must allow them to express their experience without you making it about you. If the issue is indeed about your actions or lack thereof remember that it is about *their experience*. This is not the place for "right and wrong". It is not about examining the holes in their logic where you can swoop in, point it out, and you get to be right. This is where your partner shares how they experience you. This is where they share how *they feel* inside that experience.

Understand that if you can hold the space for them to feel safe enough to fully move through their entire experience, the healing can finally come to a point of resolution. What is possible is for you to assist your partner in healing a part of them that had never before had a chance to come to the surface. This is a real opportunity for growth that is absolutely beautiful once you can get to the other side.

Part II: Relating to Each Other

> *"Understanding these key elements about how people function in the world around them will prepare you for using the framework for extraordinary relationships without guilt, shame or fear."*

In order to properly relate to each other, we need to understand one another. There are different ways in which we:

- Connect with each other;
- Give and receive love;
- Mentally process information;
- Time conversations;
- Type personality;
- React to anger;
- Access centers of the brain; and
- Perceive the world based on our sex & gender.

Understanding these differences about ourselves and our partner can begin to answer the questions of, "Why do I…" or "Why does he…?" or "Why does she…?" then fill in the blank. Understanding these key elements about how people function in the world around them will prepare you for using the framework for extraordinary relationships without guilt, shame or fear.

Connecting

There are four levels of connection: physical, intellectual, emotional, and spiritual.

Physical Connection

Physical connection can occur instantly and can deepen over time. Most people know instantly whether or not they find another person attractive enough to take action. If the interaction leads to a relationship, you will notice that the other person continues to become more and more attractive as the connection becomes stronger. If the relationship does not progress through to the other levels of connection, the expression of the physical connection could be limited to merely a sexual relationship. Over time, the chemical reactions created in the body wan and without the other levels of connection, the relationship could be in real danger of ending. These types of relationships can burn hot and fizzle out quickly.

Intellectual Connection

Intellectual connection can take a little bit of time to develop. This happens over a few interactions where dialogue is the primary focus. As the conversation organically goes to varying topics, you will begin to notice if the other person's intellect and their areas of interest match yours. While it is possible to have two people connect intellectually when there is a large gap between them, recognize that the larger the gap is the more effort will have to be put into bridging that gap. With judgments come resentments. With resentments come issues. If a person has no judgments about their own mental acuity and their partner's lack thereof, they have just moved a step in the right direction.

If there is a large gap intellectually, each person will need to find that kind of connection from friends, professors, mentors, or other people on their same level. A strategy to overcome the divide *within* the relationship is to identify common areas of interest where you can enjoy activities together. Find something that excites the both of you and spend time together creating *shared experiences*. Research the topic together. Learn something new together. Make it something special that you share. It has the potential to create a bond that will be extremely strong inside the context of the relationship.

Emotional Connection

Emotional connection takes time to develop. As the physical connection deepens and the intellectual connection provides bonding over shared experiences, an emotional connection can develop. This is when the level of significance of the other person begins to increase. You may notice that it becomes more and more important what the other person thinks. Their opinion may begin to matter greatly when it wasn't even considered before. You may find yourself thinking of them at unexpected times. You may begin to include them in your plans for the future. All of these things occur in the beginning of the relationship as feelings begin to develop.

Over time, those feelings can grow into more substantial emotions. When they are hurting, you feel compassion. You want to comfort them. It is possible to get to a place where you feel compassion for them even when they are angry and lashing out at you. When you can feel compassion for them even when they are actively trying to (verbally) hurt you, you will have reached a deeper level of emotional connection. It is possible to remain calm and recognize the anger is a reflection of their pain. When you can understand that, you will feel compassion.

When you can love the other person so deeply that you are willing to let them go so they will be happy (if that is what is required), then you have let go of your attachment to the outcome and are truly loving that person. When you can actually feel joy at the thought of them being happy even if that means not being with you, then you have an understanding of what is possible with a full emotional connection with another.

Spiritual Connection

Spiritual connection develops over a period of years. This is expressed as *shared growth*. As each person evolves as an individual and shares those experiences with their partner, the relationship itself begins to evolve. Each epiphany gained creates a spiritual connection to each other within the relationship. The dynamic nature of the relationship must be flexible enough to grow and change as the individuals experience life changing perspectives and events. Spiritual connection cannot survive in a static relationship that will not allow for change. The relationship must be fluid and *recreated continuously*.

Spiritual growth can be as difficult or as easy as you make it. Some people believe it can only be accomplished through immense suffering. Others believe they can learn the exact same lesson through laughter. *Whatever path you have chosen, that is where you will be*. The decision is yours. It is up to you how it all plays out. When you can get to a place where you share a deep and meaningful spiritual connection, you will have a relationship that is *extraordinary*.

Love Languages

Dr. Gary Chapman wrote a fantastic book entitled "The 5 Love Languages" (1992/2010). Over the course of his career, he identified five distinct ways people show and expect to receive love. He called them *love languages*. According to Dr. Chapman, a disconnect occurs when there is a gap between how we expect to receive love and how our partner actually shows us they love us. In general, people tend to show love based on how they want to receive it. However, if we can examine ourselves and our partner from the perspective of our love languages we can begin to understand each other's needs. When we can grasp what our partner needs on a fundamental level, we will then know how to give them what they need. Having this simple yet extremely profound need met can facilitate a connection that can transform relationships from surviving to thriving. With this basic knowledge, it is possible to have the kind of relationship that everyone else points to and says, "I want what *they* have!"

Words of Affirmation

Words of affirmation can take the form of emotional uplifting appreciation, compliments, words of encouragement that inspire courage, words expressed from a place of love and kindness, humble requests that affirm your partner's worth and abilities, and even lifting your partner up to others (including your children) when they are not around (Chapman, 1992/2010, pp. 37-54).

As a child, my grandfather and I were very close. Since I was the eldest of six children and his first grandchild, we had a very special bond. I often sought his approval by looking for that pat on the back that would let me know I had done something right. However, he was very quick to tell me, "I will never tell you that you did a good job unless you go so far *above* the bar you can't see it anymore. Anything less than that is what you are supposed to do anyway."

Well into my adulthood, I still longed for him to acknowledge me by telling me so. Then one afternoon, it finally happened. I received a phone call from him that touched me like no other ever has since. He proceeded to tell me all of the things he was proud of about me. He walked through all of my accomplishments one after another. He even mentioned a few things I was surprised he had even noticed. I remember noticing that he was talking fast which was unusual for him, he never did that. However, the thought soon left as I sat in my chair, tears slowly making their way down my face, relishing in finally feeling like he saw me – at last. At some point he abruptly had to end the call, apologized for having to go, told me he loved me, and he hung up. That was the last time I ever got to talk with him.

Unbeknownst to me, my daughter had gotten ahold of the portable phone and had hidden it within a pot inside the kitchen cabinet. She had turned the ringer off. A few hours later after much searching I located the lost phone. The second I turned the ringer back on the phone rang. It was my mother. She was in hysterics. My grandfather had died from a massive heart attack. It wasn't until the funeral, speaking to the people that were there when he passed that we realized he was actually talking to me on the phone when he died. He knew that he was dying and the one person in the world he wanted to call – was me. That's why he was talking fast and had been out of breath. Knowing that he had lived his entire life connecting with so many people over the years and the person he wanted to talk to before he went was me, is the greatest affirmation I can imagine. It touched me so deeply that I just don't have words for it.

I learned two things from that conversation. One, my grandfather *always* appreciated me even if he didn't tell me. He just showed it in different ways like quality time and shared experiences. Two, I became very present to how healing it is to finally be acknowledged. So now, I rarely miss an opportunity to tell someone when I appreciate them. Friends, family members, coworkers, and even strangers can always use one more reason to smile.

Quality Time

The focus with quality time is receiving undivided attention from and spending time with their partner sharing experiences. This involves focused attention, quality conversations where you can listen sympathetically and speak authentically. (Chapman, 1992/2010, pp. 55-72). Quality activities have three essential components: (p. 69)

1. At least one of you wants to do it;
2. The other is willing to do it; and
3. Both of you know why you are doing it – to express love by being together.

Quality time is my love language. I absolutely love long engaging conversations where the human endeavor can be experienced and explored. The best conversations are ones where time goes by unnoticed. Other shared experiences that excite me usually involve some sort of adventure. These can range from peaceful hikes in the woods identifying wild edibles, to swimming with the dolphins in the ocean, to adrenaline overload by jumping out of an airplane. They all add to those memorable moments where you can say, "Remember that time…?" that later define the history of the relationship.

Receiving Gifts

To some, gifts are an expression of love. It is a statement that their partner was thinking of them in that moment. Weekly inexpensive gifts can make all the difference in the world to someone that feels loved by receiving gifts. It is a visual reminder that they are important to their partner. (Chapman, 1992/2010, pp. 76-88).

My dear friend Anita has the love language of receiving gifts. She shows love by giving the perfect gift. She will spend months just listening to what you are interested in. Once she has the general topic she will spend a few weeks subtly pulling information out of you about that area. Then she will use that to go and do research to find you that personal gift that will be unique to you. She will top it off with just the right wrapping paper, matching ribbon, and card that took hours to pick out. When you receive a gift from her, it will definitely be something that has great meaning to you.

Acts of Service

Expressions of love arrive in the form of doing things for your partner (Chapman, 1992/2010, pp. 91-106). For people who show love through acts of service, they will tend to take care of all of the little details of the day. They will cook and clean for you, they will run errands for you, they will help you with your projects, and offer to help before you even realize you need it.

My grandmother showed love with acts of service by feeding you. When you walked into her home, there was a special table in the kitchen dedicated to all the yummy goodness that was unique to her. There were the staples of homemade pound cake made from my great grandmother's secret recipe, homemade coffee cake unlike any other, brownies cooked to just the right consistency, and on special occasions the added bonus of pumpkin pie and pecan pie baked from scratch – and that was just walking in the door. Meals were an event at her house. Second helpings were almost a requirement, partially because you just wanted to go back for more, but mostly because my grandmother had to ensure there was absolutely no room left in your stomach whatsoever.

Acts of service aren't my primary or even secondary love language. I've never been accused of being domestic and fully engage in outsourcing wherever possible. However, I did pick up a great love of being in the kitchen from my grandmother. To me, there is nothing more magical than cooking while the people I love are gathered around the kitchen table laughing and spending time together. I most definitely show love to the people I care about by feeding them. The simple act of preparing and sharing a meal with them brings me great joy.

Physical Touch

Love can be expressed through physical touch. At its height it can be illustrated though sexual intimacy. However, it can also be a loving caress as you sit together at dinner, a hand on the small of her back, a light kiss, and even holding hands as you walk through the garden (Chapman, 1992/2010, pp. 109-120). It's that intimate touch reserved for and found between just the two of you.

Sometimes when our partner is in crises, we don't know what to say. In those moments a reassuring hand to comfort her and a loving embrace can be the one thing she needs the most. "If your spouse's *primary love language is physical touch*, nothing is more important than holding her as she cries" (Chapman, 1992/2010, p. 113). Just being there, loving her, connecting with touch can make all the difference for a person who needs to be touched in order to feel loved.

The importance of touch is exemplified in the opening lines of the film *Crash* (2004):

> *It's the sense of touch. In any real city you walk, you know. You brush past people. People bump into people. In LA, no one touches you. We're always behind this metal and glass. I think we miss that touch so much that we crash into each other just so that we can feel something.*

What's My Love Language?

To determine your love language, go online to www.5LoveLanguages.com for free interactive profiles by Dr. Chapman. I also encourage you to read his book "The 5 Love Languages" (1992/2010). It *will* make a difference in your relationship.

Information Processing

A crucial aspect of being able to create effective communication involves understanding how the other person processes information. Neuro Linguistic Programming (NLP) provides some insight into how people process information: (Knight, 2002)

- Neuro – the way you filter and process your experience through your senses;
- Linguistic – the way you interpret your experience through language; and
- Programming – the way you code your language and behavior into your own personal program, [i.e. how you integrate it into your verbiage and daily life].

NLP can be studied for years in an attempt to understand the nuances associated with how information is processed. However, looking at just one factor of sorting styles even at a basic level can provide great insight into what the other person needs in terms of communication. The information sorting styles typically fall into eight categories: (Hohl & Karinch, 2003)

Large Chunk 1 – 2 – 3 – 4 – 5 – 6 – 7 – 8 – 9 - 10 **Small Chunk**
big picture ▲ *detail-oriented*

Sequential 1 – 2 – 3 – 4 – 5 – 6 – 7 – 8 – 9 - 10 **Random**
orderly, ▲ *juggler, productive*
process-oriented *in spite of a messy desk*

Positive 1 – 2 – 3 – 4 – 5 – 6 – 7 – 8 – 9 - 10 **Negative**
optimist ▲ *pessimist*

Sameness 1 – 2 – 3 – 4 – 5 – 6 – 7 – 8 – 9 - 10 **Difference**
looks for ▲ looks for
similarities & patterns contrasts

Present
Past 1 – 2 – 3 – 4 – 5 – 6 – 7 – 8 – 9 - 10 **Future**
oriented on: what happened ▲ tomorrow
before today

I 1 – 2 – 3 – 4 – 5 – 6 – 7 – 8 – 9 - 10 **We**
definite sense of ▲ prefers confirmation
self-worth & from others
own ideas

Polarity Responder 1 – 2 – 3 – 4 – 5 – 6 – 7 – 8 – 9 - 10 **Conformity Responder**
offers alternatives, ▲ more likely to agree
"devil's advocate" than to offer alternatives

Approach 1 – 2 – 3 – 4 – 5 – 6 – 7 – 8 – 9 - 10 **Avoidance**
actively curious, ▲ inhibited,
moves toward moves away from
the unknown the unknown

For example, let's say that Deborah is detailed (small chunk), Brian is bullet point[1] (big chunk), and Carol is chronological (sequential) in terms of information sorting styles.

Deborah (**detailed**) must tell her story with as much detail as possible. She will spend a great deal of time explaining every little facet about what she is trying to convey because she views each aspect as being vital to the other person being able to understand the entire picture. When she listens, she will typically ask a lot of questions. Deborah (detailed) is driven by the need to understand. In order to understand, detailed information is king.

Large Chunk | 1 – 2 – 3 – 4 – 5 – 6 – 7 – 8 – 9 – 10 | Small Chunk

big picture   *detail-oriented*

Brian (**bullet point**) explains just the bare minimum of what needs to be communicated in order to get the message across. It's like the Cliffs Notes (n.d.) study guide version of the great novel. When he listens, he is looking for that golden nugget of what makes the effort of listening worthwhile. He is the big-picture guy. Brian (bullet point) is driven by the need for efficiency and context is very important to him.

Large Chunk | 1 – 2 – 3 – 4 – 5 – 6 – 7 – 8 – 9 – 10 | Small Chunk

big picture   *detail-oriented*

Carol (**chronological**) feels compelled to explain things in the order in which they happened. This happened first, then that, next this, and so on. If she gets interrupted, you may observe her having to go back to the very beginning of the story and start all over again. When

---

[1] Small chunk and detailed refer to the same classification. Whereas, large chunk, big chunk, big picture, & bullet point refer to the same classification. Likewise, sequential and chronological refer to the same classification.

she listens, she needs to hear how each piece fits into the sequence of the story. She feels most comfortable if the story is told in consecutive order; however at a minimum she needs to link the segment with the proper order. Carol (chronological) is driven by order and timing is extremely important to her.

Sequential	1 – 2 – 3 – 4 – 5 – 6 – 7 – 8 – 9 - 10	Random
orderly, process-oriented		juggler, productive in spite of a messy desk

There can be a challenge when the styles of information processing are different. For instance, when Deborah (a detailed person) and Brian (a bullet point person) attempt to have a conversation without understanding each other's communication needs it could potentially end badly. Communication can breakdown and typically neither will know why.

The key is to be present to each other's needs. Deborah (detailed) is driven by understanding and an abundance of information is very important. Brian (bullet point) is driven by expediency and context is very important to him. How can the need for lots of detail and the need for "Just the Facts" where one doesn't really care about time as long as there is enough of it and the other is watching the clock, align in such a way as to give them both what they need at the same time?

The answer is communication *structure*. If the timeframe of the conversation is set beforehand, it provides enough room for Deborah (detailed) to talk as long as she needs to and it also sets the expectation for Brian (bullet point) that he should settle in and get comfortable because it may take a while. A simple question of, "How much time do you have?" sets the stage for the timeframe to be addressed right in the beginning. It gives Brian (bullet point) the option to address any potential distractions in the environment before beginning the conversation.

It does not matter which person goes first. What matters is that before the conversation starts, Brian (bullet point) is asked to have leniency for Deborah (detailed) and be prepared to answer a lot of questions that may require calling up some detail. The key is to let Brian (bullet point) explain the story in big chunks and wait until he is finished before stepping in and asking questions. Deborah (detailed) can wait. Expediency is important to Brian (bullet point), so it won't take that long. This gives him what he needs which will elicit a sense of calm within him and makes it easier for him to give Deborah (detailed) what she needs – more time and lots of details.

When Deborah (detailed) is telling a story, she needs to provide the context for Brian (bullet point). Deborah (detailed) cannot just jump into the middle of the detail without giving the other person what he needs in order to understand *how* to listen and inside of what framework. Deborah (detailed) should give Brian (bullet point) the golden nuggets and the big picture at the very beginning of the story. Brian (bullet point) needs to know upfront that there is a point to the story that is worthwhile for him. This will give him what he needs so he can relax and listen to the details of the story for Deborah (detailed) with the nuggets providing the table of contents for him.

Input versus Output

An interesting nuance is that the category of information processing may be different in terms of input and output. For example, a person that is observed as being extremely detailed when they communicate may actually *prefer* bullet points when hearing a story. Sometimes someone can be a bullet point person driven by the need for efficiency where context is very important who has *adapted* to a detailed style of communicating. This is because they process information in big chunks (input) however they believe they will not be understood without providing all of the detail another needs (output) to come to the same conclusion as they have. Therefore, when they speak, they provide a lot of detail to the listener. This is commonly found in extremely analytical thinkers. Before categorizing a person's information processing, discuss the driving forces, understand what they are listening for, and observe how they speak.

By understanding each other's communication needs and implementing a structure, the prior stumbling blocks melt away. It allows the conversation to progress to a point of new territory. Being able to go to those unexplored places with each other affords the opportunity for *real growth*. It forges a connection inside the context of the relationship that continues to grow as you delve deeper and deeper into your ability to share your life together and understand each other on a more profound level.

Conversation Timing

If you were to observe communication in its natural state, you would see there is a particular flow associated with it. There is a natural back and forth process that occurs when two people are engaged in a regular conversation. This flow is the life force of the dialogue.

In general terms, people typically have a style of flow that is on a scale between the extremes of Now or Later.

Now | 1 – 2 – 3 – 4 – 5 – 6 – 7 – 8 – 9 – 10 | Later

For instance, a person with a **Now Flow Style (NFS)** will speak the words as they are formulated. The thought is given life through voice almost as instantly as it was born in the mind. These people often talk fast because their mouth is trying to keep up with their brain. Since thoughts are thrown around inside the discussion as they appear, you will often see conversations with this style jumping from topic to topic, going off on tangents, and usually ending up at the point eventually.

Now | 1 – 2 – 3 – 4 – 5 – 6 – 7 – 8 – 9 – 10 | Later

In contrast, a person with a **Later Flow Style (LFS)** is much more purposeful about what they say. They think about not just what to say, but precisely how to say it as well. They formulate the words in their mind and run a few scenarios; testing which ones will likely have the best outcome. Then once everything feels comfortable with the exact words in the proper order they will speak. This is sometimes referred to as "radio" because of the lag time between live radio and when the sound actually reaches the listener. The lag time affords the opportunity to censor anything that may harm the show. Someone who is a LFS is essentially censoring their own words in order to protect themselves from being taken the wrong way and to also protect the listener from any inadvertent words that could potentially cause harm.

Sometimes, with a LFS there is a swirl of information in their head and they need time to make connections between those thoughts. They need to understand the context and how it fits into the bigger picture. They need to understand the inputs and how they relate to each other. It is this connection process that causes the lag time between formulating their thoughts and actually saying them out loud.

Now | 1 – 2 – 3 – 4 – 5 – 6 – 7 – 8 – 9 - 10 | Later

When both the speaker and listener have the same flow style, the conversation can feel effortless. My youngest daughter and I have been told on more than one occasion that it appears as though we have our own language. It has been described as a type of shorthand. We can bounce around from topic to topic and never miss a beat. Any topic switch is met with intrigue because something from the previous segment had triggered this new path in the conversation. It is fascinating to observe the thought process that can be discussed in its original area and then given a totally new purpose when applied to another seemingly unrelated application. These types of conversations between us are invigorating and have been known to last for hours at a time. As a mother, I truly treasure those conversations between us. They live in some of my fondest memories.

While immeasurable bonding can happen when the two styles are the same, a complete breakdown in communication can occur when the styles are different. If Luke as a LFS is speaking, Naomi as the NFS will find it nearly impossible to wait until Luke (LFS) is completely finished with a topic before saying something. This is because as Luke (LFS) is talking, it creates links in the other person's mind that they really want to share *right then*. This lands on Luke (LFS) as him being interrupted by Naomi (NFS). If the topic is sensitive, it could cause Luke (LFS) to not feel heard, he gives up, and then shuts down. This brings the conversation to a screeching halt. Luke (LFS) feels terrible and Naomi (NFS) looks around not having a clue as to what just happened.

A challenge is that Luke (LFS) will sometimes judge Naomi (NFS) as being irresponsible for just blurting out anything that pops into her mind while Naomi (NFS) can judge Luke (LFS) as being way too slow and dragging out the conversation. As a result, timing can play a significant role in a breakdown when the two flow styles are different. For instance, when Naomi (NFS) is trying to wait until Luke (LFS) is finished before speaking she will look for a pause. Unfortunately, an overzealous Naomi (NFS) may jump into the conversation when Luke (LFS) was merely taking a breath in order to continue his thoughts. Another issue with timing can come up when Luke (LFS) offers an extended pause. A really long pause can appear like an end to the topic, however it may just be a long radio session running inside Luke's (LFS) head. He may feel unsure and run various different scenarios. While it may seem like a lull in the conversation to Naomi (NFS), to Luke (LFS) there is no silence because there is an entire conversation playing out in his mind.

The difference in flow style can also show up in terms of what amount of physical and emotional space is needed when things do eventually blow up. Luke (LFS) will often need space alone to work out the problem in his own mind before he can feel safe enough to engage in conversation again. For Luke (LFS), the more time the better. Providing him with uninterrupted space allows him to come to resolution on his own. However, Naomi (NFS) solves her problem during the act of talking about it out loud. It is a collaborative effort. She wants to talk about the issue immediately so there can be instant resolution. Time away from each other could help, but usually not very often. It is the act of the conversation that provides the avenue Naomi (NFS) needs to potentially come to resolution.

Something to consider is that Luke (LFS) tends to be an extremely good listener. This is because he listens to himself in his mind before ever speaking anything out loud. He values being heard.

It is because he understands how crucial listening is to the conversation that he typically has a lot of patience and can wait until the other person is *completely* finished before taking his turn. So, when interrupting causes an issue inside the conversation, it is up to Naomi (NFS) to do the work.

The person doing the interrupting is responsible for controlling their own outbursts. Naomi (NFS) needs to understand the cost associated with the interjection.

    Interruption (NFS) →

    Luke (LFS) does not feel heard →

    Luke (LFS) gives up →

    Luke (LFS) shuts down →

    Conversation abruptly ends.

Any connection between Luke (LFS) and Naomi (NFS) breaks and ends with them feeling disconnected from each other.

The fear for Naomi (NFS) is that she will forget something that may be crucial to the conversation if she has to wait until the end to present it. One option would be to have pen and paper ready to take notes. As Luke (LFS) speaks, Naomi (NFS) could jot down a note to remind her of a question she'd like to ask or a comment she'd like to make. There is a risk that as the writing is occurring Luke (LFS) will not feel heard since it may be interpreted that a person can't effectively listen to what is being said while also writing down their own thoughts. This risk can be alleviated by having a conversation with Luke (LFS) beforehand. Naomi (NFS) could explain the reasoning behind the note taking. Explain this is an attempt to ensure no more interruptions happen because it is extremely important that Luke (LFS) feels heard. Naomi (NFS) could request that Luke (LFS) compromise a little and provide some leniency in this avenue that could potentially allow the conversation to come to a point of resolution if it is getting blocked by interruptions.

Naomi (NFS) may find that as time goes by the note taking process will aid in training her mind to stop and think before speaking. Eventually, the note taking will become obsolete altogether. Once Naomi (NFS) can connect with how profound it can be to bring a conversation completely through resolution, the need to interrupt will simply fall away. When she can truly feel connected to her partner as she works through something that had eluded them up until that point, they will feel closer to each other than before the issue showed up in the first place. The moment she *really* gets this concept and understands the impact of it, interjection will not be a factor any longer.

A Lesson in Interrupting

I came to fully connect with this one day when my partner at the time and I had a disagreement. He had gotten upset with me over something that to him was a *huge* issue while I struggled to understand why it was such a big deal. He was quite upset and while I was able to remain really calm, I just wasn't getting it. I struggled to grasp the connection between the events and his reaction to it.

We were in the car on a rather lengthy ride back to the house after a long weekend away for my birthday. Neither of us could go anywhere, so I attempted to find resolution to what had just happened. I walked through all of the stages of listening for him and we seemed to be getting somewhere. He was being extremely vulnerable with me and I was beginning to feel his anger dissipate. Then, all of the sudden the bottom dropped out of the conversation and it crashed and burned. I was so shocked. I had no idea what had just happened. It had been going so well.

After a bit of silence, I told him that I was feeling extremely stuck and that I didn't understand what just happened. I asked him to please try and explain what went wrong and to tell me what I should have done differently.

"You solved the problem," he said.

"I'm sorry... what?" I asked.

"You solved the problem. I just wanted you to listen to me. Instead you offered a solution. Even though it was a wonderful idea and you provided a really great solution, it made me feel like I wasn't heard and I shut down. I didn't feel safe anymore," he explained.

I was so confused. "By providing you with a viable solution, couldn't that be interpreted as me understanding your problem well enough to solve it? In order to solve it, I'd have to understand it. Solving it equals you should feel heard, right?"

"No, solving it stopped my thoughts about the problem. I was being vulnerable with you and by you talking; you interrupted me before I could completely walk through it to the point where I understood it myself. I've never thought about this before. I was beginning to get somewhere with it. Then, you offered a solution before I was even finished. It interrupted everything for me and I just shut down," he clarified.

I felt like I had just been hit with a ton of bricks. Instead of solving the problem, he needed me to just listen to him and hold the space for him to come to an understanding of it himself. I felt such compassion for him in that moment. I apologized for not understanding before and asked if he'd be willing to try talking it through one more time with a promise of silence from me until he was completely finished.

He had gotten angry earlier. Since all anger ultimately boils down to fear, I asked him what he was actually afraid of. When those events earlier in the day unfolded and he got angry, what fear was the anger trying to protect him from? He spent the next 45-minutes to an hour talking about his fears around the issue.

Instead of wanting to interject, the answer was so simple… just ask him if he's complete in what he wanted to say. Simple. *Just ask.* It took out all of the guess work and associated stress with possibly being wrong out of the equation. I didn't need to take notes or wait for a long pause. I just listened intently to him, felt what he was saying, *really* connected with him, became comfortable with the really long pauses, and just *asked* if he felt complete. Did he experience a shift in how he felt about the issue?

The result was an epiphany for him about the actual underlying fear that triggered the initial angry response. I finally understood the cost of my interruptions --- *I was robbing him of the opportunity to experience a life changing epiphany.* It truly changed our relationship and how we related to each other.

Default Flow Style

The flow style of communication can change depending on the state of the person's nervous system. The default style is usually present when their nervous system is in a **parasympathetic** state (rest-and-digest response) when the body is at rest and experiencing calm.

The **sympathetic** state of the nervous system is when the fight-or-flight response takes over and the person gets ramped up. Their breathing increases, their thinking becomes much quicker, and they even talk faster. Everything speeds up. This is when you could observe a person that would normally portray a LFS with extended processing time convert to what appears to be a NFS who speaks as the thoughts are being formulated. This is usually event driven. Once the event has passed and they experience calm again, they will revert back to their normal LFS self.

Another consideration is that *the default itself can change*. If a person has spent most of their life in a high stress environment, their nervous system could experience a constant sympathetic state of fight-or-flight. If they were able to address enough of the traumatic experiences stuck in their nervous system and have those events be processed and released, it could create a shift from sympathetic (fight-or-flight) to parasympathetic (rest-and-digest) within the nervous system itself. This is when you could observe a person that would normally portray a NFS who speaks as the thoughts are being formulated convert as a *new default* to LFS with extended processing time.

There are many types of body work that address trauma stuck in the nervous system; Network Spinal Analysis (Epstein, n.d.) is a technique of chiropractic, then there is Ortho-Bionomy (n.d.) and a Clearing just to name a few. In the Frequently Asked Questions (FAQ) section of the Clearing website, the following explanation is listed: (Clearing Energy Work, 2012)

When life experiences create stress (*physical, emotional, mental, chemical, or spiritual*), if the body cannot process it in the moment, that stress gets stored in the body. It is a survival mechanism created by the body so that the trauma to it can be addressed at the point in time when there are enough resources available to effectively process the trauma. Each time a new stress occurs that cannot be processed in the moment, it gets stored. Over time, there can be a significant buildup of events that become stuck in the body. If those areas are not addressed, it creates a tension pattern in the body that over time can show up as physical ailments, emotional distress, mental illness, toxicity, and spiritual stagnation.

A Clearing is a type of healing energy work that clears the areas in the body where the energy is stuck. It releases the energy blockage to restore proper flow for optimal health. This creates the condition necessary for the body to be able to effectively process the previously stored trauma thereby allowing the body to heal itself. The Clearing is a re-education of the nervous system where it can begin to learn how to operate in a state of relaxation and calm. As a result, a Clearing promotes a relaxed body, calm emotions, clear thoughts, and spiritual growth.

Myers-Briggs®

> *"Whatever the circumstances of your life, the understanding of type can make your perceptions clearer, your judgments sounder, and your life closer to your heart's desire."*
> ~ Isabel Briggs Myers

Based on Carl Jung's theory in the 1920s, Isabel Briggs Myers and her mother created a tool called the Myers-Briggs Type Indicator® (MBTI®) (Myers Briggs Foundation, 2003). The tool examines four main areas: (1) favorite world, (2) information, (3) decisions, (4) structure.

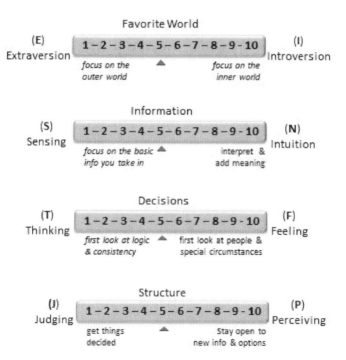

(E) – Extravert[2]	(I) – Introvert
Focus on the outer world	Focus on the inner world
Gets energy from other people	Recharges batteries through privacy
Being home alone (even when sick) is confining	Needs their own space
Now Flow Style (NFS)[3] *(See "Conversation Timing" chapter)*	Later Flow Style (LFS) *(See "Conversation Timing" chapter)*
Must experience things; easily puts themselves into new situations and environments	Prefers to observe and practice prior to experiencing something new

(S) – Sensing	(N) – Intuition
Takes the world as it is	Always reads between the lines
Looks for data	Uses their sixth sense to try to understand what is not easily seen or supported by data
Likes to build and make things; likes to use their hands	Likes innovation and creating something new
Highly organized, systematic, methodical, and realistic	Creative
Grounded and makes decision based on facts; solves problems that exist already or are attached to current technologies	More comfortable breaking the rules if it means developing something new
Views intuitives as flighty	Views sensors as unimaginative and caught up in the mundane

---

[2] Source: Briggs (1998) pp. 9-10.
[3] Original concept by the author and not attributed to Briggs (1998).

(T) – Thinking[4]	(F) – Feeling
Values the facts	Facts play a role, but not the pivotal one
Will do the research	What makes them feel good
Makes decisions with their heads	Makes decisions based on morals, values, and norms; on how they will affect people in how they feel or live

(J) – Judging	(P) – Perceiving
Planners	Spontaneous
Structured and ordered	Pile things up; cluttered
Prefer the environment to be clean, orderly, and uncluttered	Office and living space can be a mess
Deadlines with consequences	Schedules and deadlines are suggestions
Makes lists and uses them	Makes lists and lose them
Commits to a cause, goal, or calendar	Stays open; procrastinates in case new information will help with the decision; making one decision limits others; always rethinking and redoing things

---

[4] Source: Briggs (1998) pp. 9-10.

Temperament Types

Temperament types characterize the specific combination of two categories and are represented as a code with two letters: Rationals (NT), Idealists (NF), Guardians (SJ), and Artisans (SP). To understand the subtleties between the different temperament types, see the following books located under the "References" section:

- Berens (1998)
- Briggs (1998) pp. 32-35
- Kiersey (1998, May)

Personality Types

The personality type represents the preference for each category and is represented as a code with four letters. The type table reflects the 16 possibilities: (Briggs, 1998, p. 13)

	Sensing Types		Intuitive Types	
Introverts	ISTJ	ISFJ	INFJ	INTJ
	ISTP	ISFP	INFP	INTP
Extraverts	ESTP	ESFP	ENFP	ENTP
	ESTJ	ESFJ	ENFJ	ENTJ

Where "INFJ" reflects: (Briggs, 1998, p. 13)

> *Seek meaning and connection in ideas, relationships, and material possessions. Want to understand what motivates people and are insightful about others. Conscientious and committed to their firm values. Develop a clear vision about how best to serve the common good. Organized and decisive in implementing their vision.*

(See the *Appendix Myers-Briggs® Personality Types* for the complete listing.)

What's My Personality Type?

To determine your personality type:

- Take the assessment online at www.mbticomplete.com; or
- Locate a certified professional to administer the assessment and provide an interpretation for the results at http://www.myersbriggs.org under
My MBTI® Personality Type
> Take the MBTI® Instrument.

© Myers-Briggs®, Myers-Briggs Type Indicator®, MBTI®, and Personality Differences Questionnaire® are all registered trademarks with CPP, Inc. Modified and reproduced by special permission of the Publisher, CPP, Inc. Mountain View, CA 94043 from Introduction to Type, Sixth Edition by Isabel Briggs Myers. Copyright 1998 by Peter B. Myers and Katharine D. Myers. All rights reserved. Further reproduction is prohibited without the Publisher's written consent.

Anger

> "Tough is a way of not letting the soft leak all over the place."
> ~ Robina Courtin, Buddist nun

All anger boils down to fear. The anger comes forth as a protector to that piece of us that is afraid. The anger is the warrior that shields the vulnerable side of us where the fear lives. It is a defense mechanism of the body that happens without us even realizing it. The transition between feeling the fear and when the anger steps up to protect us happens in a flash. It happens so quickly that we typically don't even notice.

When you can understand that anger is merely an expression of a fear being protected, it opens the door for an opportunity of real growth. Each time anger shows up is a chance to get to the underlying fear. Being able to safely explore the fear that triggered the anger can catapult a relationship to the next level.

Self-Pity

It is important to recognize that self-pity is merely anger turned inward. In the traditional sense the type of anger we are most familiar with is when someone lashes out. The direction of travel is outward aimed at others. In contrast, *self-pity is anger directed inward aimed at the individual.* Notice when self-pity shows up, recognize it is a warning sign of anger directed inward, and begin to ascertain the underlying fear.

Toilet Seat Trigger

Howard and Crystal were newlyweds. Howard used to leave the toilet seat up whenever he used the bathroom. This used to drive Crystal crazy. She felt extreme frustration during the day when she'd walk into the bathroom and have to put the toilet seat down. However, the part that sent her over the edge was that during the middle of the night when she would get up and be half asleep, she'd forget to put the toilet seat down and she'd fall into the commode.

Howard had no intention of putting in the extra effort required to put the seat down. He said to Crystal, "I think you should be mindful of me and put the seat *up* every time you use the bathroom."

"What?!" Crystal screamed at him. "You want me to put the seat *up*? That's ridiculous!"

"No, what's ridiculous is someone putting their butt somewhere without looking first. Now, *that's* ridiculous!" The idea of Crystal falling into the commode because she didn't look first completely baffled Howard.

Crystal looked shocked. Then you could see the recognition of what he had said slowly creep across her face. She put her hand over her mouth and giggled. "I had not considered that." She laughed out loud, "I think you're right."

They then sat down and had a discussion about why it bothered her so much. Once Crystal could understand that one event could have two opposing "perspective truths" she was able to disconnect from it emotionally, zoom out, and get a clearer perspective on it. Her "truth" was that he *should* put the seat down if he cared for her at all. He *should* be considerate of her feelings. While Howard's "truth" was that she *should* put the seat up for him to be considerate of him. However, he didn't have that much of an emotional attachment to her "should" so he just let it go. It wasn't that important to him.

Howard had grown up in a house full of 13 children with both boys and girls, and he did not really care about the state of the toilet seat. Up or down. He didn't care. Frankly, he was just happy to have a bathroom. Years of military training made him thankful for simple pleasures like indoor plumbing. So why was it so important to Crystal? At first they thought that it was because she grew up in a house full of girls and that was just what she was used to. However, it didn't seem to fit. There was something missing.

He asked Crystal to explain one more time all of the details about what she experienced when she would walk into the bathroom and the toilet seat was up. Then it became clear. She said, "You should be considerate of my feelings. You should put the toilet seat down if you cared about me at all." That was it. The "*if you cared about me at all*" was her trigger. So, every time the seat was up, she interpreted that as him telling her he didn't care about her. To her, the seat up <u>equaled</u> he didn't love her.

Both of them just looked at each other as the magnitude of her fear sunk in. Howard instantly felt compassionate towards Crystal, "I had no idea that you experienced me telling you I didn't love you every time I left the seat up. Now that I see how much that really hurts you, I will make sure I put the seat down. You don't have to worry about that anymore. I do love you." He walked into the bathroom and put the seat down for her.

Crystal cocked her head to the side a little as a smile came across her face when Howard came back into the room. "You know… it doesn't bother me anymore. Now that I understand the fear and that it wasn't even real, I understand you leaving the seat up was just that – you leaving the seat up; nothing more or less than that. It just is."

From that moment on, Crystal was never bothered about a toilet seat being up. As a matter of fact, when she'd see one up it would remind her of their story and she'd smile to herself about it.

Howard never left the seat up again.

Lizard Brain

In the context of relationships, there are three primary areas of the brain that we should understand.

First, there is the **Lizard Brain** which is responsible for the maintenance of survival functions such as respiration, digestion, circulation, and reproduction (Howard, 2006). Its job is survival. It is concerned with physical instincts such as safety, sustenance, and sex (Torma, 2012). It says, "I'm hungry, scared, selfish, and horny" (Godin, n.d.)

Second, is the **Limbic System** which is responsible for activating the general adaptation syndrome (flight-or-fight response) and housing emotions (Howard, 2006). It is concerned with social instincts such as bonding, status, and play (Torma, 2012). It asks questions like, "How do I share? How can I be loyal? How can I connect?" (Godin, n.d.)

Third, is the **Cerebral Cortex**:

- <u>Sensory areas</u>: vision, auditory, and touch
- <u>Motor areas</u>: voluntary movements
- <u>Association areas</u>:
    - (back) organize sensory information
    - (front) planning actions/movement and abstract thought

This is where we have the ability to solve problems, use language and numbers, develop memory, and can be creative (Howard, 2006). The neocortex is concerned with our interpretive instincts such as meaning, morality, and making sense (Torma, 2012). It asks questions like, "How do I come up with new and cool things? How can I break tradition and challenge the status quo?" (Godin, n.d.) The prefrontal cortex is concerned with creative instincts such as wholeness, transcendence, and contribution (Torma, 2012) and looks for the lessons inside the turmoil.

Sex & Gender Differences

For an interesting scientific comparison between brain-mind functions based on sex and gender, see *Appendix Sex & Gender Differences in the Brain*. While the observations are based on statistical averages, they do provide insight into a better understanding of the differences between the male and female functions of the brain.

For example, men tend to take more interest in objects while women are generally more interested in people and faces. Men talk and play more with inanimate objects while women read character and social cues better. Men typically require more space and women require less space overall. Men have a better aural memory while women have a better visual memory. Men tend to interrupt to introduce new topics or information whereas women interrupt to clarify or support (Howard, 2006).

Men will usually solve math problems nonverbally and women tend to talk while solving math problems (Howard, 2006). This may be generalized where men have a tendency to want to be alone while working through problems in their own head whereas women will usually require a conversation to come to resolution about an issue.

Sabotage

Anytime we take on a new project or begin a new pursuit, there is a level of excitement. We imagine the desired outcome, feel what it must be like to be in that place, and see ourselves having attained that goal. It's exciting to reach into the future and observe ourselves having already achieved the objective. We rush out and buy the requisite equipment such as camping gear for our new commitment to spend more time outdoors. We pick up the latest and greatest electronic gadget to give us that little edge in reaching the goal we set for ourselves. Then we bring home our new purchases. We lay them out. We play with them a little bit imaging how much fun it will be to use them for real. Then we find them a new home in the garage or office... and they collect dust.

What happens to the level of excitement we had at the very beginning? Where did it go? Most of us have a tendency to lose excitement the moment we realize you can't win the U.S. Open tournament without spending years worth of hard work practicing on your own tennis court. Sometimes we don't realize that in order to achieve our goal, it takes some effort. We just expect the goal to walk up to us and say, "Hey! There you are. I was looking for you." For some goals, by the second or third time we run into difficulty, we bench the idea. Then we rationalize it away with, "It was too hard. I would never be able to do that. I don't have time. It requires too much effort."

What is absolutely fascinating to me is that we tend to get in our own way. According to Seth Godin (n.d.), the closer we get to fulfilling the goal, the louder the lizard brain gets. This is where we sabotage our process. The lizard brain is about survival. In its own way, it is trying to protect us. In the context of relationships, when things get too difficult or feel too comfortable (which is just "too difficult" *in waiting* to the lizard brain), the lizard brain steps in and does whatever it has to in order to make it stop.

When we begin to feel emotional, it is the limbic system that creates the emotions which trigger the fight-or-flight response. Once those emotions reach critical mass, the lizard brain steps in and says, "Thank you very much, but I am taking over now. We need to get out of here... Run!" That is when we want to abruptly end the conversation, leave the room, or get into the car and leave the house. It is our lizard brain's way of trying to protect us from a potential overload and system failure.

The key is to *not* give in to the knee jerk reaction of wanting to run away. What the lizard brain does not realize is that when there is a safe environment there is no need to shut down the discomfort. In truth, *the more emotional the topic, the higher the leverage it is to work through*. Working through that area will give you the biggest bang for your buck. If you can put the selfish need to escape aside, make the relationship a priority in that moment, and recognize that a breakthrough is just around the corner, you can get through that topic and come to a resolution. Having resolution means that you have completely worked through it; you don't have to have it rear its ugly head up at you during unexpected times when the trigger comes at you out of nowhere. When you can make a conscious choice to not repeat old patterns, you make the statement that you are willing to *stand in the fire* with your partner. This is you doing what is best for the health of the relationship in that moment instead of giving into your fears. Don't run away. Stay and talk. Say how you feel. Use the framework to get through it.

There will be resistance. There will be times when you want to run away. Decide right now that if you are going to go down this path of having an extraordinary relationship that you will *stand in the fire*. Realize that the majority of the effort will be in the beginning. You and your partner both have old patterns that will come to light. There are issues that were handed down to you by friends and family long before you even began this current relationship. Those areas come with old patterns that will have an effect on the relationship. You have to work through your old patterns before you can even *begin* to explore any new aspects created by your relationship now. However, when you can delve into the fears of the lizard brain *right now* at the beginning, the rest of the ride will become smoother the farther down the road you get.

Perseverance

> "At the moment when it appears all hope is lost, if we stand for what is possible and walk through the fear even when the challenge seems insurmountable, we can make it through to the other side. It is on the other side of our greatest fear that our extraordinary selves live."

There are but few moments that carry enough weight to stick with us our entire lives. Most merely fly by without even being noticed. Others are so heavy that they become ingrained in our everyday lives. However, for some of us, if our presence of mind is aligned with the universe and our hearts are willing to feel, something truly magical can occur. We can be privy to a miracle before us.

I'd like to share an event so impactful that it forever changed my perspective on the world. During that stage of my life, I was living in Atlanta, Georgia. It was an exciting time because the city was gearing up for the Olympics. It was as if everyone had secretly won the lottery and each person was in on it. I can't remember an era when people were more generous with their time. The current seemed to draw the most amazing people toward the center of issues that rarely even found a voice prior to this moment in time.

On this particular day, I had been invited to attend a benefit for people that were both deaf and blind. Apparently, there were eight such individuals living in Atlanta at the time. The benefit was a fundraising effort for a house specially designed with them in mind; a place of their own where they could be independent. I was fortunate enough to have a woman sitting at my table who was kind enough to answer my myriad of questions. Yes, I was that kid who constantly sat in the front of the room. I had lots of questions. I have always been fascinated with how the world works.

The woman at my table had Usher syndrome. I learned that it is the leading cause of deafblindness. She had been born deaf and because the disease afflicted her eyes, she slowly went blind. At first, her peripheral vision began to go, and the tunnel vision narrowed until there was nothing left of her sight. We communicated through her interpreter that performed sign language while touching her hand so she could feel the words being signed. It was absolutely amazing to witness. At first I was a little afraid at the completely new situation. My brain had no frame of reference, no body of knowledge from which to draw, no real clue how to navigate what was going on around me. I had always heard that when you lose one sense the others are heightened. I remember suddenly becoming acutely aware that losing two senses had the possibility of a level of distinction about the world around us that could potentially rival what science tells us. At the very least, I was certain she knew I was nervous, but she was so open with me and smiled so kindly that I found myself at ease in the conversation very early on.

I'm not sure how long we were engaged in our conversation, but at some point a woman entered the room that would change my life forever. She was tiny. Her short, curly hair was almost completely white. If I had to take a guess, I'd say she was in her late eighties. She wore a pretty, pastel summer dress with thick stockings and comfortable shoes. Someone provided her with a chair and instead of sitting in it; she pulled herself up and stood right on the seat. That alone shocked everyone in the room. Little did we know it would be the first of many shocking moments. She introduced herself as Tommie Goins. I loved her instantly. She had a way about her that you just knew she was a strong woman who made up her own rules. She was the most enthralling speaker I've ever heard.

Tommie Goins began with her story. I can't even begin to do it justice and I wish I would have written everything down the moment I got home. The details are a little fuzzy, but the effect has never changed in all these years. From what I do remember, she grew up in New York City. She was born deaf. As she explained it, it was a different time back then. At the turn of the century, people who were deaf were sheltered from the outside world. Their life revolved around the small circle of home and family; that was it. There were no friends, there was no support group around her; just a family that managed to keep their little secret locked away from the rest of humanity.

At the age of fourteen, Tommie Goins went blind. The shame of a deafblind child was more than her family could tolerate. She was taken to a section of the city she had never been to before... and she was abandoned. She had been thrown out on the streets of New York City, deaf, blind, and only fourteen years old*. We wept at the shear cruelty of the people that were supposed to protect her. Everyone at my table was sobbing; all of our hearts crushed on her behalf, devastated to even imagine how she must have felt being thrown out like that. You must remember that this was a time before government assistance, before programs were in place, before there were child advocates, before anyone ever noticed; much less cared about the death sentence Tommie Goins had just been given.

Most of us would imagine ourselves sitting down in the middle of the road with a rush of overwhelm consuming our mind and completely taking over our bodies. Most of us would succumb to the fear. We would be frozen by it. The last breath of hope would exit our bodies and we would simply... give up. Not Tommie Goins. Not only did she stand up, she reached deep down within herself and pulled up a level of strength that is astounding.

She survived and even more importantly, she lived. She lived life on her terms. She ended up going to high school, then undergrad, and in the end graduated with a master's degree in English. When I met her, she was travelling all over the country *by herself* with no one other than her seeing-eye dog. She was working for the Helen Keller Foundation recruiting interpreters for the deafblind. That was not an easy job either. She had to connect a level of giving so immense that the interpreters were willing to in essence give up their lives to be in service of another human being. In fact, many of the interpreters I met that day had families of their own that they never saw again. There are no vacations or holidays to take. That kind of job is 24/7 and it never ends. Imagine for a moment what kind of woman Tommie Goins was that she could connect the need and solution in such a way that there truly are no words to adequately describe. Merely being in her presence, feeling her words at such a deep place within my heart brought tears up that had never before seen the light of day.

Her fierce internal fortitude gave me the gift of perseverance. I learned from Tommie Goins what it means to never give up. I learned that *at the moment when it appears all hope is lost, if we stand for what is possible and walk through the fear even when the challenge seems insurmountable, we can make it through to the other side. It is on the other side of our greatest fear that our extraordinary selves live.* After having met her, each and every time I find myself begin to shut down and be afraid of what I am facing, I remind myself of her. I reconnect with her indelible spirit and tell myself that whatever self-doubt I have about being able to accomplish what is in front of me or fear that I can't come up with a creative enough solution absolutely vanishes when I remember Tommie Goins. She faced life as an abandoned 14 year old deafblind little girl all alone on the streets of New York City. If she can thrive in that kind of environment under those circumstances, I can face what I need to with my head held high. In that moment, my drive is renewed which then becomes a kick start to my will. Once I make a decision now, it is *going* to happen.

In the context of an extraordinary relationship, don't give up. Choose to have one, declare it with conviction, and then take the steps to make it a reality. When you feel like you've hit a wall, move through the fear. What is on the other side is… *extraordinary*.

***Author's Note**: *I have only been able to locate one reference to Tommie Goins by another author (Dagley, 1978), but have been unable to review the actual material in order to verify the facts as I remember them. Truthfully, I cannot remember whether Tommie Goins was born blind and later went deaf or if it was the other way around. What I do know for sure is that by the time she was 14 years old, she was deafblind and had been abandoned on the streets of New York City.*

Part III: Using the Framework

Who Do You Have To Be?

In order for the framework to be effective, there are characteristics that you will need to embody. If they do not come easily to you then be purposeful about taking them on and incorporating them into your being.

Compassionate

Allow your partner the room they need to make a mistake and self-correct. Most relationships end once the error has been identified. Then the "offender" (as a matter of perspective only) works on the solution in the interim before the next relationship begins only to have that next relationship end as soon as another issue crops up. Then they work on that problem, get to another solution, go into another relationship, and the cycle continues. Instead of ending the relationship when the problem arises, create the space within *this* relationship that is compassionate and flexible enough for your partner to do the work and find a solution. It needs to be okay for them to stumble and fall. Let them know there is room in the relationship for them to get back up again.

Courageous

When we are in physical pain or discomfort, we need to find a position of comfort for the body and move away from the pain. However, when we experience emotional and mental pain we need to find where it is uncomfortable and *step into it*.

Determine your anchor point. For example, an anchor could be that the choice has been made that the relationship will continue. When you believe the relationship is potentially over, you may be faced with the issue of abandonment. If that is a deep rooted issue for you, when that belief creeps up, everything shuts down. At that moment, there is no point in having any kind of conversation. However, if you can be courageous enough to *stand in the fire* with your partner and recognize it as merely a pattern of behavior triggered by your lizard brain, then the work can begin. So, establish your anchor and revisit it when you are afraid. *Courage is about moving forward even when you are terrified.* This is when things in the relationship can *really* shift.

Vulnerable

You become courageous by being vulnerable. You must be willing to show your partner the parts of yourself that scare even you. Be willing to explore those areas of yourself that you had sectioned off from the rest of the world due to fear. There is risk involved in shining the light on these aspects of yourself; this is true. However, it is a calculated risk. You will not be *unleashing* those areas that frighten you. On the contrary, you will merely be *observing* them and taking note of their existence and their effect on you and the relationship. You will be coming from a place of observation. *It is only when we become aware of something that we can begin to address it in a meaningful and healing way.*

Empowered

There is no room for sustained pity parties in an extraordinary relationship. While compassion is definitely in order for those moments when you or your partner are in crises, this is a short term situation. Being stuck inside a victim mentality will not allow the relationship to move forward. Make a decision right now to call each other out on self-pity when the scenario drags out for an extended period of time. Be kind, but firm. Help each other stand up again so that you both can be *real* inside the relationship and take responsibility. Sitting down in the middle of the road mired in self-pity will not move the relationship forward. It will enable the other person to continue to be a victim. Instead, they need to *stand up, take responsibility, and find empowerment* again.

Accountable

You become empowered by being accountable. Instead of blaming the other person when you get upset, you must hold yourself accountable for your reaction. It is up to you to hold yourself accountable, be willing to examine your fears as well as your hopes, identify your needs, and communicate that to your partner in a positive and loving way. *The more important the issue is to you, the more accountable you must hold yourself.* If it's important to you, you must do the work in order to move through it and get to the other side.

Authentic

When you can *speak your truth*, you will become empowered. Let go of the expectations of social norms. Let go of the "should(s)" and "should not(s)." Let go of your idea of how things are "supposed to be." Instead, get in touch with how things *really* are for you. Begin to get a better understanding of your *actual experience*. You will know you have identified your truth when you can speak about it with no judgments; when there is no emotional charge associated with it, when you can feel calm, centered, and balanced when saying it out loud.

Present

Be in the "now". If you are holding on to the past, you are *in the past*. If you are remembering something, you are *in the past*. If you are worried about the future, you are *in the future*. If you are actively planning, you are *in the future*. The only moment that truly exists is right NOW. *Be mindful about being present.* Give your partner your undivided focus and live in the moment with them.

The Upset

In the very beginning of a relationship, the need to find connection with another human being on an intimate level often gives us a filter where we only observe what will support our notion of the ideal relationship. Some of this occurs because people have a natural tendency to only present their best behavior while at the same time only being willing to see the good in the other person. Chemical reactions in the body aid in keeping this illusion alive. However, as time progresses and you have shared experiences, the filter begins to crumble and the relationship can finally begin to exist on a more authentic level.

No matter how long you have been together or how close you are to each other, there will inevitably be a situation that arises which causes some sort of upset. The upset can originate from sources inside the relationship that result from a disconnect between you and your partner. The upset could also be from emotional attachment to external sources such as friends, family, or coworkers. Either way, the effect is that your partner feels stuck in a perspective and may need your assistance in moving through the upset to get to the other side of it where they can come to resolution and find a place of calm about the situation. The best way to assist your partner is to remain calm, listen, and gently ensure the conversation moves through the framework. As the strong one in that situation, you are to hold the space mentally, emotionally, spiritually, and even physically (if appropriate) from a place of love where your partner can begin to do the work.

The person that gets upset is the one that needs to do the work. Understanding this concept is *crucial* to the effectiveness of the framework. Most people get upset and blame the other person for causing their upset. This places blame on the other person and removes all responsibility from you as the one that got upset. It creates a disconnect between you both that often results in accusations blasting the other person who then becomes defensive and things go from bad to worse.

Instead of blaming the other person, the one that got upset must hold themselves accountable for their reaction. The upset is a response to a trigger that just got pulled. Feelings are triggered. Another person cannot *cause* your feelings. They can influence them by facilitating the stimulus, but they can never cause the feelings. *Every feeling you have ever had is a need being met or not met* (Torma, 2012). The key is to get to the underlying need. In order to do that, you must hold yourself accountable, be willing to examine your fears as well as your hopes, identify your needs, and communicate that to your partner in a positive and loving way. *The more important the issue is to you, the more accountable you must hold yourself.* If it's important to you, you must do the work in order to move through it and get to the other side.

Periodic Check-In

Sometimes it is a good idea to periodically check-in with your partner to see how they are doing. There are generally four scenarios when it is desirable to check-in:

1. It's Time: The moment you realize it has been a while since you have had a meaningful conversation with each other.
2. Celebrate Successes: There is an expected success.
3. To Connect: When you feel the need to connect with your partner.
4. Under Stress: When you observe your partner may be in duress or showing signs of stress.

It's Time

Meaningful conversations can occur in less than a minute. It takes very little time to hold your partner's hand, look into their eyes, and tell them one thing you appreciate about them. Their response could be as quick as a smile and a heartfelt, "Thanks!"

It is important to understand that you don't have to block off hours of time in order to connect in a meaningful way with your partner. The moment you realize it has been a while since you purposefully connected with your partner, you should check-in with them. If you are pressed for time, offer an appreciation. If your timeframe is more flexible simply ask, "How are you doing?"

Celebrate Successes

It is important to share successes with each other. Celebrate their wins with them. Support what makes them excited and feel alive. Remember that just because something is not important to you, if it is important to your partner it matters to the *relationship*.

If you know beforehand that your partner may have the potential for a big win during the day, check-in. Did they have an important meeting? Did they pitch a big deal on the table at work? Did they land a new client? Did they finish a long-term project? Did they receive an award? Basically, anything that your partner could potentially be excited about, you should celebrate. It is the act of purposefully seeking opportunities for joy. This can add an element of fun to the relationship. Check-in with your partner and ask, "How did it go?"

To Connect

There are times when you may be missing the extraordinarily deep, complete connection you feel with your partner when you are truly connected. Whether it is because you both just got distracted with the details of the day or some unseen fear has begun to creep into your mind, the need is the same – to connect. Check-in with your partner and say, "I'd really like to connect with you. I miss you." These moments have the potential to be extremely tender and impactful to the health of the relationship.

Under Stress

Sometimes it is easier for you to observe that your partner is becoming stressed than it is for them to recognize it on their own. Maybe that potential success you were planning to celebrate actually bombed and wasn't a success at all. Maybe your partner had convinced themselves on the surface that it wasn't that big of a deal, that it didn't really matter – when in fact it did and they were feeling crushed on a much deeper level. There are any number of scenarios that could elicit a stress response. The key is to remain alert to the change in behavior.

Your partner may be very clear about what is going on and why or they may be completely unaware that anything is happening at all. Any change in their baseline behavior can be an indication of stress. This would be a good time to initiate a check-in. Ask, "How are you doing?" This will let you know your partner's level of awareness about the situation. Sometimes they may only be able to describe a feeling in their body and not have any understanding as to *why*. *(See the Appendix for the list of Feelings)*. The answer to this question will give you a better understanding of their need to vent or to be walked through a potential blind spot.

After your partner explains how they are doing, you can ask, **"What do you need right now?"** *(See the Appendix for the Needs Inventory)*. Perhaps they are in need of nurturing. There are times when people feel like they are a warrior fighting against the world. Sometimes this can be invigorating and other times it can be exhausting leaving them feeling a bit beat up. It is in these moments that they may need a little nurturing. When that happens, you can be a wonderful resource for your partner. A kind word, a tender touch, a gentle ear can make everything alright again. It's very healing to be able to walk away from the fight for just a moment and find sanctuary in your partner. It is a time when they can relax and regain their strength. Understanding what the specific need is will provide insight into how you can assist your partner with what is going on with them in that moment.

Once you can identify the need ask your partner, "**What does that look like for you?**" This will give them the opportunity to explain their request for what they would like to have happen (the action). Do not make the mistake of offering a solution in those times when your partner knows exactly what they want. If they have a specific request in mind any deviation from that could leave their need unmet. It is only when your partner truly does not know what will make them feel better that you can offer a suggestion. Even then, you must ask and see if the proposed action is a suitable fit for meeting their need. Be patient and walk them through what action would make them feel complete, resulting in a feeling of calm.

Feelings

Feelings are inner emotions or bodily sensations. They are important to understand inside the context of the framework. My relationship to feelings changed drastically over a decade ago. Although I was considered quite young for what happened, the doctors believed it was the best course of action given all of the issues that had arisen. Before I knew it, I was slated for surgery. They had scheduled me for a complete hysterectomy. For those of you not in-the-know, a "complete" hysterectomy means they remove the uterus and both ovaries.

What the doctors failed to disclose to me was the dramatic effect it would have on my emotions. When women experience menopause, it happens gradually over a period of about 10 years. This affords them the opportunity to slowly get used to the reduction in hormones, the hot flashes, night sweats, vivid dreams, and mood swings. It is nature's way of making sure everything occurs in its natural time within its normal rhythm. Unfortunately, when you have a complete hysterectomy, you are slammed into menopause as soon as you wake up in the recovery room from the surgery. I went from a regular twenty-something to a menopausal woman in the span of a few hours.

My emotions were all over the place. I opted for hormone replacement therapy (HRT) back then (now I use a natural alternative). During the timeframe it took for my doctor and I to work out the right medication at the right dosage, I was a complete mess. To this day, I am amazed any of my family and friends stayed. I once cried for four straight days. I even cried over commercials and comedy shows on television. Everything made me cry. It was horrible. After that, I hit some sort of angry phase. I yelled at anyone that got within ear shot. It truly was hideous. We refer to that time as "Hiroshima".*

In retrospect, I am extremely grateful for the experience. It forced me to examine my emotions in a way that would not have been possible otherwise. The lesson was huge. I learned that my emotions were a chemical reaction. Let me say that again... *emotions are a chemical reaction in the body.* I was shocked to realize that the origins of them were completely independent to outside influences. If I couldn't fault my emotions onto someone else and play the blame game, then that meant they were solely my responsibility. I learned that outside influences could stimulate or trigger emotions, but they could never be *caused* by them.

Understanding that feelings are merely triggered and not caused by external sources, I began to have a very different relationship with my feelings. I now use them as *indicators*. I think of them like the lights on the dashboard of my car. It's like the check engine light that tells you something is going on with the engine of your car. It's something you should look into. When I have an emotion that bubbles up, I look at it and attempt to understand the message it is sending me. It's saying, "Hey, pay attention to me. There is an insight right around the corner."

---

*Author's Note: *I mean no disrespect to the people that went through that experience nor was I attempting to minimize the impact of it on the community. This was just such an extreme time period in our lives that we didn't know what else to call it. When my eldest daughter suggested Hiroshima, we all agreed it seemed like a good fit at the time.*

Non-Feeling Warning Signs

It is not always that easy to identify and properly label our feelings. In theory it sounds simple, however in practice it can be a bit more challenging. Often times what we think are feelings are actually an evaluation, judgment, or another aspect that is not *truly* a feeling.

For example, if John came home and spent 15-minutes playing with the dog when he first walked in the door, Sarah may say she felt ignored. She expected him to by-pass the dog and seek her out instead. However, being ignored is not a feeling. It is an evaluation. John came home and spent time with the dog. That is what "is". It's just what happened. Sarah was the one that assigned the evaluation of good or bad onto his actions. Words of evaluation assign blame. She can't *feel* ignored. She can merely assign an evaluation to John's actions that result in a value judgment of ignored. Sarah can however feel lonely, hurt, and sad. Those are feelings. They do not carry with them the connotation of wrong or blame.

Beginning a sentence with, "I feel… (like, that, it, as if, you, I, he, she, they)…" is a **warning sign** that a thought, evaluation, judgment, or criticism is about to follow (d'Ansembourg, n.d.).

You can use the *Evaluations Masquerading As Feelings* list (Lasater, 2003) in *Appendix E* to determine if what you think are feelings are actually non-feeling words. Then you will be able to identify the possible needs associated with the actual feeling.

For example, when Sarah said she felt ignored, she actually felt lonely, hurt, and sad because she really needed to feel connected with John when he got home.

When You SAY:	What Might You Be FEELING?	What Might You Be NEEDING?
Ignored	Lonely, scared, hurt, sad, embarrassed	Connection, belonging, inclusion, community, participation
Rejected	Hurt, scared, angry, defiant	Belonging, inclusion, closeness, to be seen, acknowledgment, connection
Unheard	Sad, hostile, frustrated	Understanding, consideration, empathy

Needs

Every feeling you have ever had is a need being met or not met (Torma, 2012). The key is to get to the underlying need. Let's examine needs and get a better understanding of what they are.

According to Abraham Maslow (1954 / 1987), needs fall into five basic categories of:

1. Physiological
2. Safety
3. Love & Belonging
4. Esteem; and
5. Self-Actualization

Maslow indicated that there is a hierarchy of needs where the base need must be met before a higher level need can be addressed. For instance, if a person is hungry and worried where their next meal is going to come from, they are less likely to care about respecting other people. The immediate need of hunger takes precedence over the need to be a nice person and conform to social norms.

Maslow's Hierarchy of Needs

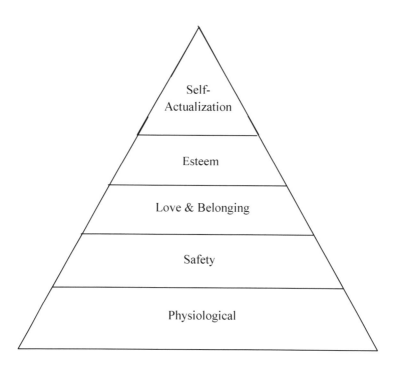

Physiological	breathing, food, water, sex, sleep, homeostasis [a], excretion
Safety	security of: body, employment, resources, morality, the family, health, property
Love & Belonging	friendship, family, sexual intimacy
Esteem	self-esteem, confidence, achievement, respect of others, respect by others
Self-Actualization	morality, creativity, spontaneity, problem solving, lack of prejudice, acceptance of facts

Note. [a] Regulation of conditions such as temperature and Ph levels.

Manfred Max-Neef (1992) expanded on Maslow's concept and differentiated between needs and satisfiers. He identified nine fundamental human needs:

1. Sustenance
2. Protection
3. Affection
4. Understanding
5. Participation
6. Leisure
7. Creation
8. Identity; and
9. Freedom

Max-Neef applied four further categories to needs that once applied aid in a person being true to one's self (authenticity):

a) Being
b) Having
c) Doing; and
d) Interacting

He then created a matrix of the needs (*See Appendix F for the complete matrix*) and filled in each field (point of union) with something that would satisfy the need (satisfier). While Maslow listed food and shelter as physiological needs, Max-Neef stated food and shelter are *satisfiers* for the *need* of sustenance.

Satisfiers serve the purpose of empowerment. For example, the fundamental human need of understanding is categorized as:

Fundamental Human Need	Being	Having	Doing	Interacting
Understanding	Critical conscience, receptiveness, **curiosity**, astonishment, discipline, intuition, rationality	Literature, **teachers**, method, educational policies, communication policies	Investigate, study, experiment, **educate**, analyze, meditate	Settings of formative interaction, **schools**, universities, academics, groups, communities, family

Here, the <u>function</u> of the satisfier:

- "curiosity" is to empower *being understood*.

- "teachers" is the empowerment in *obtaining* an *understanding*.

- "educate" is to empower the *doing* of *understanding*.

- "schools" is to empower the *interaction* of *understanding*.

A satisfier may simultaneously contribute to meeting multiple needs at the same time. For example, the satisfier intimacy, functions to empower the interaction of both needs of affection and leisure. The satisfier self-esteem, empowers being the needs of freedom (being free), identity (being known), and affection (being affectionate). Similarly, the satisfier work, empowers having (the needs for) protection, participation, creation, and identity.

Mirror

When you are in a relationship, the other person becomes your **Mirror**. They will reflect back to you how you are showing up in the world as well as how you are feeling about yourself. Observing small children interacting with their parents highlights this concept. For example, as a parent, if you are feeling anxious, your child will pick up on this and mirror that feeling that you have. They could cry if they are an infant or have a nasty tantrum if they are a toddler. An older child could lash out at you. This is because they are picking up on your emotion and reacting to it based on the environment. The emotional skill set of a child is undeveloped which is why the effect can be seen so plainly.

Adults on the other hand have learned many ways to mask this effect. The direct effect is hidden underneath a complicated set of misdirections; it is still there nonetheless. You just have to know how to look for it.

You Don't Appreciate Me

When you are feeling unappreciated by your partner, examine that feeling. First recognize that "unappreciated" is not actually a feeling. It is an *evaluation* of possible feelings of "angry," "hurt," or "frustrated." (*See Appendix: Evaluations Masquerading as Feelings*). Understand the feelings are in response to *unmet needs* which could be appreciation, respect, acknowledgement, and consideration. When you have a need of appreciation that is not being met, you can feel hurt.

Second, ask yourself if you are expecting *your partner* to fulfill that need for appreciation? Be gut-wrenchingly honest here. Have you made a condition of the relationship, that your partner appreciates you? Do you have an *unspoken expectation* that your partner will appreciate you? Do you have an *internal rule* that is already in place, that says when you don't feel appreciated, it is your partner's fault? If you are unsure of the answer, ask yourself if you blame your partner for not appreciating you? If you have assigned a judgment of "blame", then the answer is "Yes."

Realize that your partner may be appreciating you in their own way. When you create a rule that makes your partner responsible for you feeling appreciated or not, you assign certain conditions to that rule. You may decide that you have to be *told* you are appreciated. This sets up a condition of pass/fail. When your partner does not expressly state they appreciate you, they fail. What if your partner *does* actually appreciate you *greatly*? What if they have a pattern of reticence since childhood? What if they have a belief that it is not safe to verbalize acknowledgement of their feelings in the context of appreciation? What if they show you in actions instead? Do they constantly show you they love and appreciate you by taking care of the details of the day? Do they go out of their way to do that little something special? Do you notice? Do you acknowledge it?

Once you can understand the condition you placed onto the relationship, you must now be accountable for that action. Now grasp the concept that the statement of "You don't appreciate me" is actually an external manifestation and reflection of your internal self-judgment of "*I don't appreciate me.*" Think about your life. Examine the areas where you do not appreciate yourself. Ask questions like:

- Am I hyper critical of myself?
- Do I have a host of judgments about myself?
- Do I acknowledge my own gifts?
- Do I celebrate my own successes?
- Do I take care of myself?
- How do I demonstrate that I love myself?
- Do I love myself?
- Do I believe I am worthy of love?
  - From me?
  - By another?

Examine these areas where you may not be appreciating your own self. If you have never considered this before, be kind to yourself. Being accountable is good news because you can take responsibility moving forward. All you have is right now. The past cannot be changed. It just is. Empower yourself to recognize the warning signs as they arise and walk through these questions to get to the other side.

You Don't Take Care of Me Financially

Bret and Linda had been in a relationship long enough to begin to merge their lives. The physical attraction was off the charts, the intellectual connection was extremely strong. They were both intelligent with their own respective areas of expertise that they gladly shared with each other. Virtually all of their interests were shared. What excited one, almost always excited the other. They loved doing things together. They viewed each adventure as an exploration of what made them happy. Their spiritual connection was growing daily. Both were focused on personal growth. As one learned a valuable lesson, they shared it with the other and the relationship grew stronger as a result.

Linda had come from a corporate environment and because of a layoff was reexamining her chosen path. She was trying to figure out a way to be more present, tap into her gifts, encompass a measure of fulfillment into her potential work and explore her options. Linda was plagued with fear about her financial future. She vacillated back and forth between trying to create a future that was everything she ever dreamed of and giving into fear and returning to the corporate world. Bret was extremely supportive. He talked with her for countless hours helping her design what would be the perfect way for her to support herself. He had owned successful businesses before and was trying to impart some of his wisdom to shorten her learning curve. She tried different things out and Bret was always right there for her.

Then one day Bret walked into Linda's office and with a panicked look on his face asked for her help. His key person had just quit with no notice. She had been his right-hand-(wo)man from the inception of his latest company. He had relied so heavily on her that her leaving was a devastating blow. Bret asked Linda to step in and fill her shoes. Linda was filled with compassion for Bret. Her nurturing side would have done anything for him to make his hurt go away. He needed her and she was more than happy to drop everything and help him.

Over the next two months, Linda worked tirelessly on making sure his business kept afloat and that the customers did not notice that anything had changed. There were many nights when after Bret had gone to sleep, she would get up and work until dawn on his company only to slip back into the bed as the birds were chirping in the morning. Even on her birthday because Bret was feeling unsettled about the state of his company, she worked for five hours just so he would feel a sense of calm, that everything would be okay.

The more that Linda did for Bret, the more he asked of her. The time commitment was increasing and it left her no time to work on her own projects. She made a conscious decision to put everything of hers on hold while she helped Bret. She witnessed her bank balance dwindle and as she missed her first mortgage payment and overdrew her checking account at the bank, she began to panic. Then she remembered that Bret had told her that he wanted to share everything with her. He had told her that he was more than happy to take care of her when the business was in a position to create those kinds of funds because excess was not important to him. Bret said that as long as he had enough money to pay the bills, the rest could be used for them to create a life together and have the freedom to travel. He said he was more interested in quality time with her than hording money in the bank. So Linda reasoned that she wasn't really working for Bret, she was actually working *with* him. She believed in that moment that her financial future was best served by building Bret's company *together*. With Linda's expertise she felt certain she could help Bret reach that goal much faster with her than without her. She believed they were *creating a life together*.

Then there was a blowup. Bret's company experienced a devastating blow. It completely blindsided Bret and sent him reeling. He felt like his world came crashing down around him. His anger reared up in intense protection mode of his fears that were running rampant throughout his body. In response, he lashed out at Linda and blamed her for the state of the company. He exploded and told her that she didn't have his back. He told her she had been responsible for that area therefore she had created that situation *on purpose*. He immediately fired her and broke up with her. There was no discussion. Bret had decided and that was that.

Linda was baffled. How could Bret say such a thing? She felt like Bret didn't "see" her. It told her that he didn't know her at all. Anyone that did know her would know she would *never* do anything like that! She was mortified at the thought of losing him. He was the first man she had ever been in-love with. She had loved people before, but this was the first time she had ever been truly *in-love* with another person. The anguish that overtook her consumed every fiber of her being. She told him that he needed to pack up his stuff and be gone by the next afternoon. She was going to go to her friend's house for the night. She knew he loved her and his pattern was that he'd get angry, he'd calm down, they'd talk about it, and then everything would be okay. Linda just wanted Bret to fully comprehend the magnitude of his decision. She wanted him to see what an impact his words had. However, she never expected him to *actually* do it.

Early the next morning, Bret texted her and wanted to reconcile. By this time, Linda was so overcome with grief that she could see no possibility of feeling anything other than pain. She was so absolutely destroyed by being thrown away like a piece of trash that she told him she loved him and did not want to be in relationship with him any longer. She spelled out a few of the reasons leaving the most egregious ones to herself. She wanted him to understand that if they were to get back together, he could never just throw the relationship away again unless he really meant it. The path of destruction was too wide within her heart to bear it again. She didn't think she'd survive another blow like that. Linda had *no intention* of ending the relationship. She just wanted him to understand how badly he had hurt her.

Then Bret sought council from one of his best friends, Tina. It just so happens that Linda had mentioned to Bret *the day before* about her serious concerns regarding his friend's involvement in his company. Linda had shone the light on Tina's shortcomings in Bret's business. This was the very same person that now had a personal agenda to get rid of Linda. Linda was threatening her friendship with Bret as well as her financial position. Tina told him to pack up and leave Linda that she wasn't worth the effort. She told Bret he was better off without Linda and he believed her. Tina had already picked out Linda's replacement for Bret and couldn't wait to put those wheels in motion. So he rented a U-Haul, packed up everything including the items that he had given Linda as gifts, took food out of the pantry and left her.

When Linda returned home, she looked around the house and she was overcome with the emptiness of it. She collapsed on the bed and screamed a guttural, heart-wrenching scream into her pillow over and over for two hours. It was only when her throat became swollen and she could physically no longer scream that it stopped. She had never felt so heart-broken in all her life. The tears just wouldn't stop. She thinks she even cried in her sleep.

Later that evening when Linda woke up she went downstairs and sat in the kitchen. She held her head in her hands and began to cry again; this time from fear. Bret knew that she had a negative bank balance. He knew she only had about $3 in change at the bottom of her purse and no work on the horizon. How was she going to make it through this? She didn't have a credit card to get by on. She had nothing. She had never been so completely broke before in her life. She had no money for gas in the car. She had no money for groceries. How was she going to feed her daughter? Linda looked around and was shocked that Bret did not at the absolute very least leave her money for food and gas. Not one cent. How could he do that? How could he just leave her with nothing like that? She felt betrayed by him. She had given him everything she had – opened her home to him, given him her heart, all of her time, she had taken care of him, and shared with him the absolutely most precious thing in her world - her daughter. Linda had never before allowed another person to "take care of her." It was such a stretch for her that she felt a level of betrayal that she could not adequately describe. Her heart was broken and for this piece it was because she had no way to take care of her daughter.

Insight

Linda blamed Bret for not taking care of her financially. However, she had never actually conveyed her expectation to him. In fact, until he left she was not even *aware* that she had the expectation at all. She had freely given everything she had to him and did it gladly. It was not until he left that in retrospect all of it had been a sacrifice. Linda now realized that she sacrificed her financial future to help someone else. Bret did not stay and fight for the relationship. He gave into his own fears and allowed his lizard brain to take over. Linda realized that she had not been authentic with Bret. She said things she didn't mean. She told him to pack up and leave – she didn't mean it. She told him she no longer wanted a relationship with him – she didn't mean it.

Linda eventually came to the realization that it was not up to Bret to take care of her financially. She had made the decision to put the rest of her life on hold for him. She did that, not Bret. In examining the external manifestation of "Bret didn't take care of me financially," she saw the reflection of her internal self-judgment of "*I don't take care of me financially.*" When Linda could own up to the fact that she was accountable for her own financial situation, she no longer felt betrayed by Bret. She no longer held the title of "victim" at his hands. She understood that she had done it to herself. It brought her some level of peace to no longer blame him.

Over time this made her feel calm because even though Bret had left her, she still loved him deeply. She loved him enough to want him to be happy even if that meant he was away from her. She understood that he had given into his fears and she felt enormous compassion for him. It brought her peace to no longer hold any anger or ill feelings for him. She was finally able to forgive him – *completely.*

When Linda was able to forgive Bret, she began to wonder what *his* mirror had been. In examining the external manifestation of "Linda doesn't have my back," she saw the reflection of Bret's internal self-judgment of "*I don't have my own back.*" On a very deep level, Bret was upset with not being able to take care of himself. The external manifestation of "Linda hurt the company on purpose," was a reflection of Bret's internal self-judgment of "*I failed my own company.*" She felt enormous compassion for him once again. Linda sincerely hoped he would find a way to forgive himself regarding the judgments he had placed on his own actions although they had been running in the background and most likely without any awareness at all.

Learn from Bret and Linda's story. Your relationship does not have to end in order for you to have an insight that could save the relationship when it is on life support. When you can relieve the pressure you have unwittingly placed onto the relationship, you may just find that your partner freely gives that which you desired. And if they don't, you will see how to fill that need yourself. Either way, it frees the space up inside the relationship for it to be *extraordinary*.

Children

If this is a new relationship and you already have children, consider having an age-appropriate conversation with them about the possibility of a new person coming into the picture. *Children* should always be the highest priority – period. When you bring someone new into your lives, there is an impact. How you handle the introduction of this potential partner will set the tone for that integration process.

Initial Dating

Before introducing this new potential partner into your life with your children, consider taking time to simply date and get to know that person. Evaluate them to ascertain their worthiness relative to your children. If they seem like a keeper, then observe how you are together. Do you mesh well? Ask yourself if this potential relationship will enhance your life or detract from it. See if your *wants* around the relationship match up with the *needs* of your children.

Pre-Meeting

If you determine that this person you are dating is someone that is going to be an actual partner and that it is time to introduce them to your children, have an age-appropriate conversation with the kids first. This is a *crucial conversation* to have with them. Use the learnings from this framework to have a meaningful dialogue. Converse back and forth; this is not the time for an announcement that a decision has been made. You should consider possible feelings and needs that your children may have around the topic. Find out what they need and ask what their requests are. Often, children are *told* what will happen next. If they are included in the decision making process, it creates the ecology where they are given permission to have a voice. This can be an incredibly powerful gift to a child.

Initial Meeting

If you have decided to move forward with the initial meeting, take the time to determine the best environment. Would it be better to meet in your home where the children feel the most comfortable? Your partner could be extremely nervous too. Remember that this is scary for them also. They should feel comfortable as well. Would it be better to meet in a neutral location like a park or a fun event? Selecting the right environment for that very first meeting is important. Take the time to plan well.

What you say or don't say is entirely up to you and your threshold for what works for you in that moment. What you should be aware of though is how you both are showing up. Are you nervous? Kids pick up on that and it could make them feel uneasy. Are you being authentic? Are you showing vulnerability? Do you have compassion for all of the people involved; the big ones *and* the little ones? As the adults, you are setting the tone. You are accountable for ensuring a safe environment for the kids to be able to express themselves. Remember to breathe, relax, and just be (a PG version of) yourself.

During the Relationship

Make a concentrated effort to periodically check-in with your kids to see how they are experiencing the relationship. How is it affecting them? What is their experience? Ask them what they see. That simple question could provide you with surprising results. Regardless of their age, children observe *everything*. You would be amazed at what they catch on to. While I will caution you to not take absolutely everything they say literally, I do believe what they say should be strongly considered. It is about their experience. It's important information to take into account.

If you are going to make your children the priority, they must be included in the conversation. Many times children will keep their opinions about the relationship to themselves if they are never expressly asked. Consider this story about Linda, Christine, and Bret. Linda and Bret had been dating for quite a while before the relationship came to a screeching halt and ended abruptly. While they were not actually living together, over time Bret had managed to move a large portion of his belongings into the house. He would stay in their home for weeks at a time. To Christine, Linda's 13-year old daughter, it felt like he was indeed living with them.

It wasn't until Bret had moved everything out of the house that Christine finally confided in Linda what she thought about their relationship. Christine said, "Remember a few months ago when we were all eating dinner and I formally asked Bret to be a part of our family?" Linda remembered. To her, it was incredibly touching that her daughter would love Bret enough to on her own ask him to be a part of the family. Linda knew exactly what conversation Christine was talking about.

"Well, after I said that to Bret, he never reached out to me. Not one single time after that did he even attempt to connect with me. He didn't try at all." Christine was visibly hurt by thinking about it. She had been carrying that around for months and never said a word.

Linda reached over and placed her hand on Christine's arm, "You know what, I didn't even notice that. Now that you mention it, you're right. I can't believe I didn't see that before. I'm so sorry you were hurt by that."

Christine continued, "And you know what else… he was mean to you. He was moody and had a trigger temper. I didn't like the way he treated you at all." After a long pause she added, "He was really selfish. I can't tell you how many times I was actually shocked at how selfish he was. I expect that from my friends. They are just kids and don't know any better, but a grownup? It really confused me. Worse than that was what it did to you. I saw that it made you sad."

Linda's heart sank. In that moment she realized what kind of message she was sending to her daughter about how relationships were supposed to work and most disappointingly how a woman is supposed to be treated by her partner. It was not what Linda would have chosen as lessons to impart on her daughter about relationships. She was going to have to really take stock on this one. There were serious lessons to be learned.

Christine turned her head to the side a little, "Didn't you notice that I mostly stayed in my room when he was here? At first I was trying to give you guys space because I knew you liked spending time together. Then after a while, I just stayed in there to not have to watch how he treated you."

Christine gave Linda a big hug, "I know you're hurting right now, Mom. He didn't just leave you. He left me too. I know you miss him, but I'm glad he's gone. Maybe now you can get back to your old self."

Linda fought back tears, caressed her daughter's cheek, and asked, "Why didn't you ever say anything?"

Christine whispered, "Because... you never asked."

Stages

There are four distinct stages that occur when the other person is speaking: initiation, free flow, clarity, and resolution. Understanding each stage gives the listener the opportunity to create the conditions necessary for a successful outcome.

Initiation Stage

The initiation stage begins when the speaker indicates they need to talk. Sometimes, this will be stated clearly and other times it may be subtle. As the relationship evolves, you will begin to see the enormous value in these conversations and the need to tip toe around initiating will fall away. The fear of beginning the conversation will eventually be replaced with the fear of *not* having the conversation at all. It is when the dialogue stops that the relationship gets put on life support. The process of moving through the dialogue is what will heal the disconnect between you. It is the vehicle that will bring you closer to each other than you were before the issue got on your radar screen in the first place.

Often times, the speaker will have spent time thinking about the topic for quite a while before they approach you about holding that conversation. This usually finds you in the middle of an activity when your partner wants to talk. You will have to determine the priority of the situation and decide to stop in the middle of what you are doing or if you need just a few more moments before beginning. The speaker may be extremely afraid of having the conversation, so keep this in mind. It will be up to you as the strong one in that moment to prioritize.

If you need more time, ask if it can wait five-minutes while you wrap up so that you can completely focus. Wrapping up should include creating the opportunity for the conversation to last however long it needs to. Prepare the environment. If you were listening to music, watching television or a movie, turn them off. If you were on your computer, shut it down. Lock the front door so any drop-ins will go away. Turn your phone's ringer off (not just on vibrate mode). Remove any potential distractions from the environment so you can focus on what is really important.

Decide where you want to be during the conversation. For me, being outside in nature has an almost immediate calming effect. There is something quite healing about being surrounded by life in the great outdoors. If there is water nearby, then even better. However, if the idea of a bug landing on your arm causes a great deal of stress for you, then perhaps forego being outside. Find the area within your environment that you go to in order to feel calm. Be mindful of your partner's comfort zone as well. Are you at home in the garage covered in grease while your partner prefers a sterile Petri dish in their laboratory? The key is to find that location where you *both* feel comfortable. If you are home, would sitting next to each other on the couch work for this topic? Would a pile of pillows on the floor be better? Would it be more comfortable to stretch out on your bed while you both communicate? The ability to sit in a comfortable environment helps with the external piece of creating an internal safe space for the speaker.

Once you decide on the appropriate location for the conversation, ask your partner if that area works for them. Typically, if you have chosen a place that consistently has a calming effect on the both of you, your choice will stand. If not, reevaluate and make another selection. What takes minimal effort on your part can create enormous gratitude in your partner around the location selection. It communicates to your partner that what they have to say matters and that you are making the relationship a priority.

While you are going through the process of wrapping up and making the location selection, begin to mentally prepare yourself for the conversation. Make a conscious choice to come from a place of love. Notice if there is any tension in your body, breathe, and let it go. Begin to relax your body so that you can feel calm.

Free Flow Stage

Once you both are in the appropriate location for the conversation, get comfortable and then allow the speaker to start talking. Let them say whatever they need to. Just let them talk. A very long time ago, a dear friend of mine, Dr. Fred Blum said, "*One of the greatest gifts you can give to another person is your focus.*" Your undivided attention can be extremely healing for your partner. Listen to your partner. Focus on what is being said. Your job is to look them in the eye (even if they won't look at you), hold a safe space for them to talk where you have no judgments, and you just listen.

Remember that the issue is not always about you. Let me say that again... *the issue is not always about you.* Sometimes, the person speaking really just needs you to be there as a friend to listen to them and love them through their challenge. There are issues that come up that are a personal struggle for the speaker unrelated to the relationship. However, whether your partner is just beginning to feel the emotion bubble up or they are deeply mired in a full blown crisis, there will be an *effect* on the relationship. Listen.

If the issue is indeed about your actions or lack thereof remember that it is about *their experience*. This is not the place for "right and wrong". It is not about examining the holes in their logic where you can swoop in, point it out, and you get to be right. This is where your partner shares how they experience you. This is where they share how *they feel* inside that experience. This is where you listen. Just listen.

You as the listener must be open to criticism. One of the greatest benefits that can often show up as one of the greatest challenges is that when you are in relationship you are a mirror for each other. Your partner will reflect back to you exactly how you are showing up in the world. Those places that you do well in can illicit appreciation from your partner while the areas you struggle with or are blind to can produce criticism. There are times when it is extremely difficult to accept our weak spots. Recognize that this mirroring effect from your partner is indeed a gift. It is

a gift of insight and it is being given to you by someone that cares for you deeply enough to stand in the fire with you. Remember that if you can approach the criticism from a place of love, the insight is just around the corner. It is how you as the listener can hold the space of open and honest communication that has integrity. Your willingness to just listen without judgment will create the safe space required for the healing process to begin in the relationship.

Notice if the speaker is looking at you or not. Often times, they will begin talking while looking at something else like the ceiling, out the window, or on the floor. This has to do with how they process information. Looking up indicates your partner is seeing a "movie" in their mind about what they are explaining to you. Looking to the side means they are hearing something such as their internal dialogue while they were attempting to understand their thoughts or perhaps they are remembering a past conversation. Looking down shows you that they have great feeling around what they are saying.

As their story progresses, you may observe changes in where the speaker looks. Some aspects will have a stronger impact, illicit greater feeling, and you will notice where the speaker was once looking upwards (seeing the internal movie of the event) and they shift their gaze towards the floor. Be especially kind and thoughtful in those moments when your partner looks down. This may be the time to reach out and hold their hand or brush the hair away from their face. It acknowledges their feelings and communicates that you care.

If your partner had begun looking elsewhere, notice when they look at you again. This can be a clue to you that either the small piece of what the speaker is saying has concluded and they are now moving on to the next subject or perhaps their side of the conversation has now ended. They

may be completely finished and have said everything they needed to when they look at you accompanied with a long pause. Listen and wait a little while longer just to be sure. Then ask if they are complete; have they fully expressed themselves?

Clarity Stage

The clarity stage is where you both will do the work. The purpose is to get clear on what is *really going on*. This is where the magic happens. What a person is upset about or has strong emotional connection to is rarely what is really going on underneath the hood. It takes exploration to get to the core of the issue. Put your courage hat on, hold each other's hand, and go for it.

The work that you do will be dependent on the issue that comes up. Begin with identifying the feelings (see the Feelings chapter). Then identify the unmet need (see the Needs chapter). The following suggestions have been included to address specific unmet needs as well as those that can apply to any situation. (**Note**: *This list is not intended to be all inclusive. It is merely provided for a direction of inquiry*.) Finally, follow-up with the request (see the Request chapter) even if the request is of yourself.

Unmet Need	Suggested Application	Section
*Any	Ask for What You Need	Requests Chapter
	Evolution	Evolution Chapter
	Judge-Your-Neighbor Worksheet	Exercises
	Nonviolent Communication Model	Exercises
	Periodic Check-In	Periodic Check-In Chapter
	Perseverance	Perseverance Chapter
	Sabotage	Lizard Brain Chapter
	The Upset	The Upset Chapter
Acceptance	Leave the Judgments Behind	Requests Chapter
	Outside Influences	Outside Influences Chapter
	Positive Perspective	Exercises
Acknowledgement	Perception Pie Chart	Exercises
	Words of Affirmation	Love Languages Chapter

Unmet Need	Suggested Application	Section
Appreciation	Appreciation	Exercises
	Words of Affirmation	Love Languages Chapter
	Perception Pie Chart	Exercises
	You Don't Appreciate Me	Mirror Chapter
Awareness	Accountable	Who Do You Have To Be? Chapter
	Authentic	Who Do You Have To Be? Chapter
	Determine What You Want	Requests Chapter
	Disagreement Postmortem	Disagreement Postmortem Chapter
	Evolution	Evolution Chapter
	Present	Who Do You Have To Be? Chapter
Beauty	Appreciation	Exercises
	Positive Perspective	Exercises
Caring	Perception Pie Chart	Exercises
Celebration of Life	Positive Perspective	Exercises
Challenge	Courageous	Who Do You Have To Be? Chapter
Choice	Choice	Choice Chapter

Unmet Need	Suggested Application	Section
Clarity	60-Day Fear Challenge	Exercises
	Anger	Anger Chapter
	Authentic	Who Do You Have To Be? Chapter
	Disagreement Postmortem	Disagreement Postmortem Chapter
	Evolution	Evolution Chapter
	When I Say…	Exercises
Closeness	Authentic	Who Do You Have To Be? Chapter
	Love Languages	Love Languages Chapter
	Perception Pie Chart	Exercises
Compassion	Attachment to an Outcome	Requests Chapter
	Authentic	Who Do You Have To Be? Chapter
	Compassionate	Who Do You Have To Be? Chapter
	Self-Pity	Anger Chapter

UNMET NEED	SUGGESTED APPLICATION	SECTION
Communication	Disagreement Postmortem	Disagreement Postmortem Chapter
	First Domino	Crucial Conversation Chapter
	Perception Pie Chart	Exercises
	Personality Types	Myers-Briggs Chapter
	When I Say…	Exercises
Connection	Authentic	Who Do You Have To Be? Chapter
	Connecting	Connecting Chapter
	Love Languages	Love Languages Chapter
	To Connect	Periodic Check-In Chapter
Contribution	Bring a Solution	Requests Chapter
	Empowered	Who Do You Have To Be? Chapter
Empathy	Information Processing	Information Processing Chapter
	Conversation Timing	Conversation Timing Chapter

Unmet Need	Suggested Application	Section
Growth	Accountable	Who Do You Have To Be? Chapter
	Authentic	Who Do You Have To Be? Chapter
	Disagreement Postmortem	Disagreement Postmortem Chapter
	Evolution	Evolution Chapter
	Spiritual Connection	Connecting Chapter
	Vulnerable	Who Do You Have To Be? Chapter
Harmony	Outside Influences	Outside Influences Chapter
	Positive Perspective	Exercises
	Wellbeing	Wellbeing Chapter
Hope	Positive Perspective	Exercises
Inclusion	Prioritization	Crucial Conversation Chapter
Integrity	Core Values	Crucial Conversation Chapter
Joy	Celebrate Successes	Periodic Check-In
	Positive Perspective	Exercises

Unmet Need	Suggested Application	Section
Love	Emotional Connection	Connecting Chapter
	Love Languages	Love Languages Chapter
	What Really Matters?	Universal Truths Chapter
(To) Matter	Perception Pie Chart	Exercises
Meaning	Spiritual Connection	Connecting Chapter
Recognition	Love Languages	Love Languages Chapter
	Perception Pie Chart	Exercises
Security	Core Values	Crucial Conversation Chapter
	You Don't Take Care of Me Financially	Mirror Chapter
Safety	60-Day Fear Challenge	Exercises
	Anger	Anger Chapter
	A Lesson in Interrupting	Conversation Timing Chapter
	Sabotage	Lizard Brain Chapter
	Safe Space	Crucial Conversation Chapter
	Under Stress	Periodic Check-In Chapter

Unmet Need	Suggested Application	Section
Self-Expression	Empowered	Who Do You Have To Be? Chapter
Sexual Expression	Physical Connection	Connecting Chapter
	Physical Touch	Love Languages Chapter
Stimulation	Intellectual Connection	Connecting Chapter
	Wellbeing	Wellbeing Chapter
Support	Celebrate Successes	Periodic Check-In Chapter
	Outside Influences	Outside Influences Chapter
	Prioritization	Crucial Conversation Chapter
	Empowered	Who Do You Have To Be? Chapter
Sustenance	60-Day Fear Challenge	Exercises
	Anger	Anger Chapter
	Wellbeing	Wellbeing Chapter
Trust	Core Values	Crucial Conversation Chapter

Unmet Need	Suggested Application	Section
Understanding	Ask for What You Need	Requests Chapter
	Determine What You Want	Requests Chapter
	Disagreement Postmortem	Disagreement Postmortem Chapter
	Evolution	Evolution Chapter
	Personality Types	Myers-Briggs Chapter

Resolution Stage

At this point, the speaker should feel heard. You as the listener should mentally check in with your own feelings. Ensure you are still coming from a place of love.

Resolution begins with you as the listener. The speaker has expressed what they needed to. You then asked questions to gain clarity on what your partner said. Now it is your turn to make statements of your own if you were not able to reach resolution at the conclusion of the clarity stage. At its beginning, resolution should look like you providing a perspective that will help your partner. Is your partner holding onto a self-limiting belief (*see the Positive Perspective exercise*) that does not serve them? Is that belief different than how you know your partner to be? Have they forgotten how wonderful and amazing they really are? Are they coming from a place of fear? Can you help them see the same scenario from a place of love? If your resolution is coming from a place anywhere other than from love, wait. Think about it, reframe it, and then present it to your partner.

A **reframe** is necessary when you have taken a mental snapshot of your partner and hold them in that light even after other experiences occur. When the snapshot is stronger than the subsequent actions, you hang onto it. A reframe is the choice to take *another* snapshot and see them in a different, more empowering way. If you are having a difficult time finding a reference point for another, more positive snapshot then ask your partner how they would like for you to see or remember them for this duration.

Remember that what your partner just shared with you was extremely difficult and it exposed their inner self making them unbelievably vulnerable in that moment. Be kind. Be gentle. Come from a place of love.

Sometimes, the resolution stage can be extremely challenging. For me, I find it quite easy to listen to my partner when the topic is about anything other than me. I can listen for days, have enormous compassion,

and intuitively know the right thing to say at exactly the right moment even if that means saying nothing at all. However, when the topic revolves around something I have done wrong (even when it's just my perception), I want to interrupt even though I understand the cost, I instantly get defensive, and I generally say the wrong thing. I have found that when I am struggling with holding a safe space without judgment for my partner when they are speaking, I tend to mess up the resolution stage unless four things happen.

First, I acknowledge those pieces my partner highlighted about my actions that they were right about. There is no point in denying something that has merit. If I am wrong or if I had done (or not done) something that landed wrong on my partner, I admit it.

Second, I apologize for hurting my partner. There has never been a time when I purposefully caused harm. Ultimately, I want them to be happy. I in no way want to be the cause of any pain or misery. I want to be part of the safe haven where love lives. So, I apologize.

Third, I thank him for shining the light on a blind spot for me. Without the conversation, I would have had no idea how my actions were landing on my partner. *Awareness is the first step in the ability to make a change.* So, I am grateful for the awareness and appreciate my partner for their courage in bringing it to my attention and for their belief in me that I can show up in the relationship as my true self. It reminds me that by virtue of the dialogue itself, my partner believes it is worth the effort, believes in the relationship, and believes in my ability to make a change.

Forth, this is usually where I feel stuck and have no access to any insights or lessons to impart on my partner to help them. So, I acknowledge that I feel stuck and don't know what to say.

What is required in that moment is compassion. Both of you must be able to genuinely feel compassion for each other. The speaker has exposed their inner most thoughts and feelings making them incredibly vulnerable. You as the listener have just heard something that may be

extremely difficult to hear. Your emotions are raw. You may feel exposed and vulnerable as well.

Acknowledge how brave your partner was for speaking their truth in spite of their fears about doing so. Think about your partner when they are at their best. Imagine them in that light. See them there. Feel what it is like to observe them in that place. Then tell your partner something you appreciate about them. It will reconnect you with how you actually feel about your partner. This will help to shift the tone of the conversation from being stuck without possibility to a positive place where anything is possible.

Continue the dialogue until you have reached a place of resolution. You will know you are there when you both can think of the issue without an emotional charge attached to it. Where once the topic brought a flood of emotions, now it is simply like viewing a movie. It just is. You will have stepped into the realm of an extraordinary relationship without guilt, shame, or fear when you actually feel *closer* to your partner than before the issue arose.

Requests

Communicate to your partner in terms of requests. Covey (2000) teaches us the concept that there are two circles in which we operate: concern and influence. The circle of concern is where people have little to no ability to affect any aspect of the situation, e.g. weather. The circle of influence is an area people can have an affect such as what is seen with their health when they eat well and exercise -- or not. What's important about Covey's concept (2000) in the context of relationships is that we only have control over ourselves. We control how we react to external stimuli such as interaction with other people. However, we cannot control other people or how they react to us. We can merely influence others. We can never control them. They decide. They choose. It is up to them how they respond to us. Therefore, we cannot exhibit control over our partner by making demands or issuing ultimatums. We can merely make a request.

Determine What You Want

Ask yourself, "What do I want?" You know, it's such a simple inquiry and yet many people struggle with that very question. We spend so much of our time doing what we have to do that we forget to look up and notice our wants. Single mothers exhibit the epitome of this concept.

Adara had been happily married once upon a time. However, life happened and at some point she found herself a single mother of a toddler. She worked three jobs. Two fulltime jobs and one part time job so that her daughter could live in a safe neighborhood. Starting all over again meant that purchases had to be made with priorities in mind. Shoes for her daughter or a purse for herself? Toddlers learning how to walk, grow fast. Shoes it was. She could just staple the pieces of her ripped purse together from the inside and no one would even notice. A book on numbers for her daughter or shoes for herself? Learning was crucial at that age so it couldn't wait. A book it was.

She could just use a black marker to cover up the places that had rubbed off of her shoes and no one would even

notice. A jacket for her daughter or socks for herself? Wintertime was cold where they lived. A jacket it was. You can only wear one pair of socks at a time. Adara once went five years without buying one single piece of clothing for herself and she didn't even notice. It would be many more years before she realized that so much time had gone by.

There were only two forks in their home. One pretty one that Adara's grandmother had given her and another one she couldn't quite remember how it came to be a part of the family. Every meal, she would cook dinner, set the table, and give her daughter the good fork. Adara was aware that her daughter had no concept of a good fork versus a bad fork – but she knew. So she gave it to her daughter when she set the table – every single time. No one noticed and it didn't matter that it wasn't acknowledged. She knew.

When life becomes about doing what is required without recognizing what we want, we lose the ability to create our own life. People can accomplish amazing things when they go after a goal they really want. They just have to figure out what that is.

Leave the Judgments Behind

The more open minded you are, the freer you will become. The first step to achieving this is to be judgment free about yourself.[5] Are there parts of yourself you section off and hide? If so, why? What are you afraid of?

Mona spent most of her life showing people only the parts of herself she believed they could handle. This person could see this part and that person could see that part. Over the years, she had become so good at compartmentalizing her many facets that she realized she had groups of friends and colleagues that fit into one bucket or another, but never more than one. She wasn't exactly sure how she had come to this place, but it was exhausting keeping up with who got to see what.

She finally realized that sectioning off pieces of her was a fear-based conversation. When she sat down with her colleague, Mike, they discussed the topic. She respected him greatly and if anyone could provide some perspective, it would be him. Mike's reaction was shocking to her. He asked Mona, "Who are you to decide what I can and cannot handle? Frankly, that's more than a little insulting that you would think I would judge you like that." She was surprised by his reaction and he brought up some really great points over the next few hours. It made her realize that the judgments she was feeling were judgments she had about herself.

Over the next few months, Mona examined all the ways she judged herself. She systematically worked on each one until she could get to a place of resolution. This process lead her to an amazing discovery about herself that she had never been willing to look at before. She realized that self-judgments with work, friends, and family were merely layers to the onion. Once she could peel back all those

---

[5] Let me be clear. This is not an all-expense-paid, do-not-pass-go, free pass to do whatever you want. You are still responsible for your own actions. What is possible though is for you to have the opportunity to address those all-encompassing negative outlooks you have about yourself that do not serve you.

layers, she was able to identify a self-judgment she had previously been blind to – her sexual desires.

Mona was finally able to explore what she wanted sexually without any negative, emotional, internal conversation. This freed her up to the point to where she could have a dialogue with her partner and authentically ask for what she wanted. This is what she said:

Behind closed doors, I am very open-minded. I have <u>zero judgments</u> about what makes people tick. If you tell me you need to squish bugs to get off, I'd say, "Let's go hunt some bugs!" There are many things I really enjoy, a few things I am curious to try, and other things that are hard limits for me. However, there are <u>no judgments</u> if you want those things for yourself. So, anything that is not a hard limit for one or both of us is fair game. It's pretty simple that way.

It allowed Mona and her partner to begin to have a conversation about a topic they had never truly discussed before from the core of the onion. Neither one of them had ever expressed their wants or desires for fear of being judged by the other. As a result, their fantasies could never even hope to come true. Needless to say, after that crucial conversation, Mona's sex life was catapulted to the next level. Not only were some of her fantasies fulfilled, brand new ones were created in the process of collaboration with a willing and loving partner.

Attachment to an Outcome

When you make a request from your partner, it needs to be just that… a request. You cannot be emotionally attached to the outcome. You must give them the option to give you what you are asking for – or not. It needs to be okay for them to hear your request and choose not to give it to you.

Part of a healthy dialogue between you and your partner involves creating the space that is safe enough for you to have an

authentic conversation (*see Part 1: Crucial Conversations – Safe Space.*) Just as
you would ask for your partner to hold the space for you to feel safe enough to divulge your inner thoughts and share your request, you must give your partner the safe space for them to decline your request. This safe space is how you can have a conversation where you get to find out what about your request is impossible for them to give, merely uncomfortable, not available right now but possible in a different timeframe, and any other nuance of aspects delineating why they cannot give you what you ask. This safe space can house the dialogue for the negotiation making it possible for everyone to come to terms that work for all involved.

When you truly, deeply care for another person, you don't want to disappoint them. You want to give them what they need. You just need to make sure you are not asking them to give something to you at the detriment to themselves. If it is something they cannot give, do not ask it of them. Certainly do not hold it against them either. *Don't add something to yourself that takes away from them.* From an authentic place, allow them the opportunity to decline your request.

Bring a Solution

In general, people have no trouble communicating what isn't working for them. No trouble at all. We feel a sensation in our bodies that is less than perfect, we look over towards our partner, and then it begins – the blame game. Have you ever wondered why your partner isn't thrilled every time you "need to talk"? You need some kind of resolution, right? You need to feel better and they need to fix it, right? Who *wouldn't* want to hear that everything they do is wrong? I mean, really? Do you seriously believe your partner just sits around all day long and merely waits for you to point out all the little things they did to screw up?

Most people want to please their partner. They want to see them happy. They feel genuinely happy themselves when their partner is happy. When you point out what they do wrong, the underlying message is, "You disappointed me." After the initial guilt and subsequent feeling of disgust they feel towards themselves for having let you down, if their self-preservation does not kick in to the point where the conversation spirals downward to a word-vomit grave, they take a deep breath, look up, and ask, "Okay, now what?"

This is the point where most conversations hit a brick wall. You've made your point, they now see what they did "wrong," they feel horrible and now they want to make it better. Hello? They are listening. You have their attention. What do you do now?

Well, first let me say that it doesn't have to even go that way. It's possible to communicate in a way where your partner is not left feeling horrible in the first place. You've already learned about being accountable and how to define your feelings. You've already learned about identifying what you want and how not to have judgments or be attached to the outcome of your request. Now you must understand the fundamental concept of bringing a solution.

Before you even ask to have a conversation with your partner about what isn't working for you, there must be a clearly defined solution. It's relatively easy to say what's wrong, but now you must explain how to make it better. Bring a solution to the table.

I was once in Brussels, Belgium receiving training for a financial application a company used. I needed to understand their homegrown IT system so I could see what data was available for me to analyze. With that I could develop a continuous monitoring program for their finances to address the risk for corporate fraud.

The kingdom of Belgium has three official languages: Dutch, French and German. They have a host of other regional languages as well. So, when the company assigned an instructor to my class of two, language was a factor in how the information was communicated. I only speak English. Bobby knew the financial package inside and out. He spoke English relatively well, so he was the logical choice.

IT systems have an inherent level of complexity. Accounting for a public company has its own level of complexity. This is especially true in a global company with 165,000+ employees and many, many different operating companies across multiple industries. Therefore, it was extremely important that concepts were conveyed with the proper meaning.

Bobby had a brilliant solution. He put his hands up as a way to focus my attention on his face. He would look me right in the eye, lean forward a little, move his hands slightly back and forth, and slowly say, "Pay attention. This is important." It was amazing because there was no question that I really needed to understand that concept. That was the point to make sure I asked all the questions I needed to in order to ensure I fully understood.

I learned that in relationships there are times when our partner is trying desperately to communicate something to us that is extremely important to them. However, we don't always fully grasp just how important that piece is to them. So, my standing solution to when my partner is not feeling heard by me is to request they focus my attention.

The complaint needs to be accompanied by a solution.

When my complaint is: *When you stop talking to me, I feel sad. I need to feel close to you and connected with you.*

The solution request is: *When you are upset with me, would you be willing to sit me down, take my hands in yours gently, look me in the eye, and say, "This is important. I really need for you to hear me right now"?*

I move at an extremely fast pace sometimes. Okay, well actually most of the time I'm moving at warp speed; basically the speed of light on steroids (C^3). When my partner is trying to say something to me, there are times when I need them to slow me down and help me to focus on the fact that they have a need which is not being met. This predefined set of instructions is designed to help me be present. Once put into motion, I instantly realize I need to not just slow down, but to stop and pay attention.

Finally, there may be times when you are having an extremely difficult time coming up with a solution. This should be the exception and not the rule. However, it does happen. When it does, let your partner know that you are so stuck that you are not able to identify a solution. Try to develop a solution together. Actively try to figure out what would work to address the underlying issue. Work on the solution together. Coming up with solutions takes practice; the more you do it, the easier it will become and the closer you will be to each other.

Ask for What You Need

No matter how hard we try, there are still times when our raw emotional state overrides our intellectual self. Our heads are saying, "There is no point in being upset about this. You are overacting and on the verge of doing something foolish. Stop it now or you will regret it."

However, our five-year old emotional state retorts to the calm and all-knowing intellectual self, "I don't care! The world is crashing down around me and I need something to change right now!"

The key in that time of panic is to understand what it is that we need in that raw and vulnerable moment. What can your partner do right then that will work 99% of the time to meet that need of yours that has you running for the door or retreating into that internal little black box where no one can get to you? When you are panicking, you need help and your partner is the strong one. Here is the amazing part... you can ask for help before you ever get to that point. When you are in the midst of the panic swirl, your intellectual brain shuts down. You aren't capable of a calm and rational request. So, you should ask for what you need when you are calm, *before* the panic takes hold of you. Plan ahead. Talk with your partner. Ask for what you need at the beginning of the relationship.

For example, Irena has abandonment issues. Her father left the family when she was merely six-months old. Her mother remarried another three times. When she was just a teenager, her grandparents obtained custody of her at which time her mother told her she was no longer her daughter and she left. It was years before she was heard from again. Her first stepfather was the only person she ever considered to be a parent to her. She loved him dearly. Around that time, he was arrested on drug charges and spent several years in prison. Later as an adult, her husband abandoned her and their daughter three days after her second birthday. He just never came home; no note, no phone call, nothing. He just disappeared. Irena believed that all of the people who were supposed to love her and take care of her abandoned her. At one time or another, they all left her on her own.

This created a deep-rooted fear of abandonment in Irena. It showed up in relationships every time there was a disagreement or an argument. First, she would feel devastated at disappointing her partner. Second, she would feel unworthy of their love and affection because she had let them down. Third, she would emotionally detach and wait for them to leave. This was her pattern that she couldn't seem to get away from. It happened every time.

Disagreements are going to happen. It's not possible to be in a relationship with another human being where everything is perfect all the time. That is an unrealistic expectation. So, what should Irena do when the inevitable happens?

Irena identified her destructive pattern, understood the underlying issue it was based upon, and then devised a set of actions her partner can perform to help bring her out of the panic when it hits. With her new relationship, she had an authentic, critical conversation about this topic in the beginning when things started to look serious. Once she realized this relationship was going somewhere, she made her request:

"When we have a disagreement and you see me detaching and becoming distant or giving up, I need to hear you say, 'I am not angry with you. I still love you. I still want to be in a relationship with you.' Please only say it if/when you feel it, but if it is true for you, I *really* need to hear it."

This simple request gave her partner the tools they needed to help when Irena needed it the most.

Another example of asking for what you need can be seen with William. Most of William's childhood was spent trying to please his

father. His father was a business owner and treated his son as if he were an employee that he didn't like very much. The relationship was a lot of
orders being barked out accompanied by the always dreaded litany of reasons why William was a disappointment to his father. The conversations were completely one-sided. William was never allowed to speak. On the rare occasion that he tried, his father would invariably interrupt him telling his son what he had to say was not important.

In relationships, this created hypersensitivity towards being interrupted as well as a deep need for William to be heard. The moment he didn't feel heard, he was ready to throw in the towel and head for the door. If his partner didn't listen to him or worse yet interrupt him, he took that as evidence that she wasn't the *One* and he would be wasting his time if he stuck around any longer. It was time to cut his losses and move on.

However, as luck would have it, William was finally in a relationship with someone who actually did listen to him. Anna listened to the struggles he had with his father and how it affected their relationship even now. She identified William's destructive pattern, understood the underlying issue it was based upon, and then devised a set of actions she could perform to help bring him out of the panic when it hit.

Anna realized that when they had a disagreement, William needed to feel heard. She decided that when they would discuss the issue, she would acknowledge when he was right. It was not possible for him to always be wrong. He was a smart and caring man who had a lot to offer. He had a unique perspective and she learned a lot from him. So, when he was right about something, she acknowledged it. Giving in to even a small point by acknowledging when he was right made all the difference in the world to William. When Anna could do that from a genuine place and without any attachment to the outcome, she could see the physical reaction in William; his shoulders relaxed, he would exhale, his eyes would soften, and his entire demeanor would become calm. His need had been met. He felt heard.

Anna tested her theory a few times in true scientific fashion just to be sure. Once she had consistent results, she shared her findings with William. At first he felt manipulated; like she was just trying to get something over on him. However, as she continued to explain he began to realize that it came from a place of truly loving him. She was trying to give him something that would meet a deep seeded need within him. He began to realize that this was an unselfish and meaningful gift. He finally grasped the importance of what she had given him.

Wellbeing

Your wellbeing has a dramatic effect on how you show up in relationships. Wellbeing has multiple aspects that are interrelated: physical, emotional, mental, and spiritual. If your body is not healthy, your emotional state will suffer thereby having an effect on how you interact with your partner. What effects one aspect of our bodies affects other aspects too. When our physical body is sick or our emotional state is depressed, our mental state becomes slowed. When there is a dramatic effect to one or more aspects of ourselves, our spiritual self can begin to suffer as well. Taking care of your relationship begins with taking care of yourself.

I teach my daughters that people deal with stress in their lives in one of only a few ways. First, some people try to numb the pain. This typically shows up like addiction such as alcoholism & drugs, eating disorders such as anorexia or bulimia, careless spending such as gambling or excessive shopping to name only a few. Second, looking for or participating in affairs outside the relationship. Third, this can show up like overachieving such as becoming a severe workaholic or the compulsive unhealthy volunteer where they must help others but to the detriment of themselves. Fourth, any other destructive behavior. All of these unhealthy options are people seeking answers outside of themselves. Another option to deal with stress is to exercise. Moving your body always improves your mental state. You feel better emotionally and your body becomes healthy in the process.

Your physical body needs the proper amount of water, healthy food, exercise, and sleep. Libraries of books have been devoted to each of these topics. I suggest you do some research to devise a plan that will best support your wellbeing.

Outside Influences

Be mindful of what you say to people outside of the relationship. You must balance the desire to get help when you are struggling with a relationship issue versus holding the space for your partner to show up in a positive light to your friends and family. What you say to them will affect how they support the relationship (or not).

This is not to say that you should hide all the "bad stuff" from those who are the closest to you; not at all. However, you need to be aware that if all you ever do is complain about your partner, that is all your loved ones hear. Their natural inclination will be to support you against any foreign influences, e.g. your partner. They love and adore you. They will always (okay, 99.9% of the time) take your side. They feel this is a divine right; to stick up for you.

This will work for you when things in the relationship are bad, but what about when you work through that issue and everything is okay again? Assuming this is a long term relationship, there will be ups and downs. Life happens in cycles. Think of it like a circle. When things are bad, you are on the downturn. At some point, you will be at the bottom of the circle. Things can't get any worse than this. If you hang on long enough, you will be on the upturn of the circle. Things start to get better. Then at the top of the circle, things are at their best.

Then inevitably something happens and the cycle starts all over again. All relationships have this dynamic. What makes a relationship worth hanging onto is the shape of the circle and the timeframe of the cycle. Do you spend the majority of the time at the top of the circle or near the top? Do the snags in the relationship happen rarely and only last for a short period of time? Some relationships cycle every few years; others are volatile and cycle every few days.

Now, if we assume you are in a healthy relationship[6] then you need to be mindful of what you say to loved ones. Be sure to balance the challenges with the positives. Remember that you are creating the filter through which they see your partner. You determine what they know about them, what they see about them, what they feel towards them. What you say has the greatest impact on their opinion.

---

[6] It's important to talk to friends and family about challenges you have if they are capable of providing good and healthy advice; otherwise get a therapist. Sometimes friends and family can help you see patterns where you may be in an abusive relationship. Even abusive relationships have a circle. The honeymoon stage will always come after the beating or emotional violence. However, they cycle faster over time and you spend far more time at the bottom of the circle. Abusers tend to slowly chip away at their victim to where they can scarcely recognize their selves. Over time, the abuser will isolate their victim denying them access to friends and family. If anyone verbally or physically accosts you and you notice that fewer and fewer loved ones are around you, talk to someone. There is help available.

Disagreement Postmortem

Even relationships that appear perfect from the outside have disagreements from time to time. They are a natural part of any relationship. If the relationship involves human beings there will be disparities. What wins you the label of *healthy relationship* is how you handle that disagreement.

Once the dust has settled from an issue that has been resolved, you should take the time to reflect on the experience. Talk about it together and identify lessons learned. Ask questions to determine what went right and what went wrong:

- What went well that we should keep doing?
- Was the outcome better than expected?
- How many risks did we take?
- Did we try out new exercises or approach brand new territories?
- Where did the wheels come off?
- What didn't work about that?
- How could we have handled that differently?
- How will we choose to handle that scenario going forward?

Having an understanding of what worked and what didn't allows you the opportunity to adapt and overcome issues that could arise in the future. Implementing changes from these insights is what will allow the relationship to evolve and grow.

Evolution

Relationships are dynamic. People who actively seek knowledge, understanding, and who are purposefully finding ways to improve internally grow over time. It's a natural progression of their quest. When the individuals change, the relationship must adapt as well. Each new insight, each new lesson learned is an opportunity to strengthen the relationship. The relationship itself must be allowed to evolve.

A dear friend of mine had this to say about relationships:

Relationships are at the core of life. We are related to all things. We have a relationship to the air, water, earth, animals, insects, trees, birds, and people. These relationships are essential to our being. If one of them is off, we are not balanced. As we stand in all four-directions, we are connected to Earth, our Creator and our heart is one. We are in total strength, total balance in total harmony with every relationship all around us. We are at total peace.

~ John Scott-Richardson
Haliwa-Saponi

Life Lessons

This work does not only live inside of conflict. You can share life lessons in a conversation with each other when there is no conflict at all. You can share a lesson learned from your past or you can impart an insight that you just learned that day. All around you, the world has wonderful ways of providing opportunities for you to grow.

Important lessons can come from unexpected places. Think of the lessons we learn from the tree. A tree teaches us to be **grounded**. Its roots go deep into the earth. The tree's intimate relationship with the earth is what provides it with all of the nutrients it needs from the soil to grow strong. The depth of that relationship (how far down the roots go) determines the strength of the tree. The mighty tree also teaches us the gift of **flexibility**. When the wind blows, the tree must bend. Otherwise it will break in half. Its very survival depends on its ability to be flexible when faced with strong opposition which can come from any direction at any time.

Other lessons can come from people around you just being who they are in their natural state. When I transferred to upstate New York as a non-traditional student for my junior year of undergrad, it was more than a little scary. On my first day of classes, my eldest daughter was just starting high school and my youngest was going into kindergarten. My daughter was closer in age to the other students than I was. Being over 30 when everyone else was 20, I was often confused with the professors.

None of that was as scary though as when I graduated. I was faced with trying to find a place to live without having a job yet, absolutely no money whatsoever, and two daughters in tow. That's when two angels masquerading as humans stepped up and offered to let *all of us* live with them until we could get settled. Apparently you can't adequately fill out a job application if you don't have an address. Having lived in the car only a few years before when I first became a single parent, I was intimately familiar with the "rolling address". The angels gave us an address, a warm bed, a roof over our heads, they fed us, watched the girls when I went on job interviews, helped them with their homework, and held my hand when I felt defeated. They were my cheering section when I finally landed a wonderful job and supported us throughout the transition. We stayed with them for four months until I could save enough money to get us a small little apartment. They even helped us move. When I asked them for guidance on what I could possibly do to repay them for their kindness, this is what they said:

> *"You don't owe us anything at all. We love you. All we ask is that one day when you are in a position to, we hope that you would do the same for someone else."*

From those wonderful angels, I learned **generosity**. They will never know how much of an impact that simple statement has had on me all of these years. I believe that it altered the fabric of who I am as a person. I will be forever grateful to them both.

This book has been written from the perspective of romantic relationships. However, these principles can be easily translated to other important relationships in your life. It reminds me of one of my favorite quotes by Marianne Williamson (1992):

> *Our deepest fear is not that we are inadequate. Our deepest fear is that we are powerful beyond measure. It is our light, not our darkness that most frightens us. We ask ourselves, Who am I to be brilliant, gorgeous, talented, fabulous? Actually, who are you not to be? You are a child of God. Your playing small does not serve the world. There's nothing enlightened about shrinking so that other people won't feel insecure around you. We are all meant to shine, as children do. We were born to make manifest the glory of God that is within us. It's not just in some of us; it's in everyone. And as we let our own light shine, we unconsciously give other people permission to do the same. As we're liberated from our own fear, our presence automatically liberates others.*

Text from pp. 190-1 {"Our deepest fear... liberates others."} from A RETURN TO LOVE by MARIANNE WILLIAMSON. Copyright © 1992 by Marianne Williamson. Reprinted by written permission of HarperCollins Publishers.

Part IV: Exercises

Use the following exercises as a way to become closer to your partner. Some of them you can do alone for yourself or for your partner, and others you can go through together. If you take these assignments very seriously, you may just find that a few of them are absolutely life changing.

Appreciation

In general, people tend to gloss over the good. For some reason we feel compelled to communicate when things are not working for us; however we typically do not take the time to tell our partner when we appreciate their efforts. You can change that.

The Love Letter

Take the time to go out and get (or use) nice paper. Use a good pen; it's important. Sit down in a place with no distractions; inside or outdoors, whichever provides the best inspiration. Think about your partner. Bring forth that feeling you have when you feel *truly connected* with them. Handwrite a love letter to your partner. Let them know you "see" them. List all of the things that you appreciate about them. Tell them all the reasons you love them. Acknowledge their strengths. Tell them how you *feel*.

Favorites

Every evening, share with your partner the favorite parts of your day. *Really* connect your partner with the joy you felt in those moments of experiencing your favorite parts. Now, communicate *at least* one piece that includes your partner. What aspect of your favorite part of the day involved them? Let them know that they brought you joy. I encourage you to do this on a daily, weekly, and monthly basis. Think back over the course of the month and share your favorite parts of it with you partner. Be sure to include their part as well. *Shared joy can be very healing.*

Perception Pie Chart

Sometimes the *perception* of a partner's actions and what gets *communicated* about the experience are two different things. When people feel frustrated they often find themselves focusing only on the source of the frustration many times to the exclusion of anything else. This is when people have a tendency to exaggerate the negative and minimize the positive attributes of their partner or the relationship itself.

For example, if I only tell my partner when they mess something up and never tell them when they do something right, my partner may believe they never do anything right. If I appreciate something about my partner and never tell them, they may never know that I see them in that positive way. If the only time I communicate is when something is wrong, my partner may believe they are not appreciated when in fact they are. Use this exercise to determine if what you are experiencing, what you are communicating, and what lands on your partner, are the same.

Instructions:

Where there are two people in the relationship, Natasha and Jose:

Part 1

1. **Chart A** (internal reaction): Natasha fills out Chart A based on her internal reaction to Jose's behavior.

2. **Chart B** (external reaction): Natasha fills out Chart B based on what she communicates (verbal and non-verbal) to Jose about his behavior.

3. **Chart C**: Jose fills out Chart C based on what he experiences when Natasha communicates his behavior to him.

Part 2

4. **Chart A** (internal reaction): Jose fills out Chart A based on his internal reaction to Natasha's behavior.

5. **Chart B** (external reaction): Jose fills out Chart B based on what he communicates (verbal and non-verbal) to Natasha about her behavior.

6. **Chart C**: Natasha fills out Chart C based on what she experiences when Jose communicates her behavior to her.

Your Partner's
Total Actions in One Day

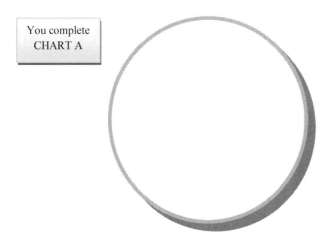

[red]	You react to with frustration	%
[yellow]	You don't notice	%
[green]	You really appreciate	%

1. Fill in the red piece of the pie on the circle representing the percentage of the day where you reacted to your partner's actions with frustration. List the percentage on the table.

2. Fill in the green piece of the pie on the circle representing the percentage of the day where you really appreciate your partner's actions. List the percentage on the table.

3. Fill in the remaining part of the pie on the circle with yellow representing the percentage of the day where you didn't notice your partner's actions. List the percentage on the table:
(100%) less (red %) less (green %) = (yellow %)

Your Total Communication About Your Experience of Their Actions

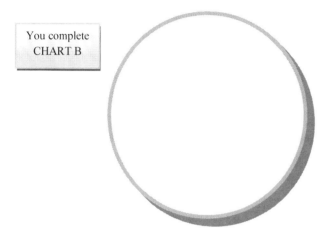

[red]	You react to with irritation	%
[yellow]	You don't communicate	%
[green]	You really appreciate	%

1. Fill in the red piece of the pie on the circle representing the percentage of the day where you communicated that your partner's actions caused you frustration. List the percentage on the table.
2. Fill in the green piece of the pie on the circle representing the percentage of the day where you communicated that really appreciate your partner's actions. List the percentage on the table.
3. Fill in the remaining part of the pie on the circle with yellow representing the percentage of the day where you didn't communicate your partner's actions. List the percentage on the table: (100%) less (red %) less (green %) = (yellow %)

What You Believe Your Partner Observes About Your Total Actions in One Day

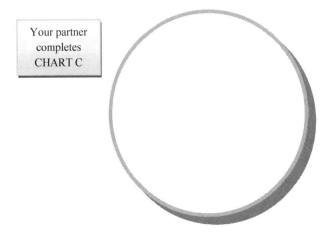

[red]	They react to with frustration	%
[yellow]	They don't notice	%
[green]	They really appreciate	%

1. Fill in the red piece of the pie on the circle representing the percentage of the day where your partner reacted to your actions with frustration. List the percentage on the table.
2. Fill in the green piece of the pie on the circle representing the percentage of the day where your partner really appreciated your actions. List the percentage on the table.
3. Fill in the remaining part of the pie on the circle with yellow representing the percentage of the day where your partner didn't notice your actions. List the percentage on the table:
(100%) less (red %) less (green %) = (yellow %)

Sample of an Exaggeration

Your Partner's Total Actions in One Day

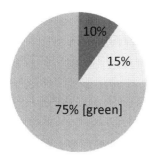

CHART A (internal reaction)

This is what you <u>observe</u> about your reaction to your partner's behavior.

Natasha's general reaction to Jose

Your total communication about your experience of their actions

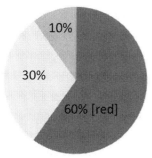

CHART B (external reaction)

This is what you <u>communicate</u> to your partner.

Natasha's communication to Jose

What you believe your partner observes about your total actions in one day

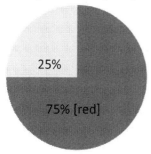

CHART C

This is what your partner <u>experiences</u>.

How Natasha's communication lands on Jose.

Interpretation

<u>Exaggerate</u>

When you observe less frustration than you communicate (the observed % of frustration is less than the communicated % of frustration), it exaggerates the extent to which you are actually irritated with your partner. When we are angry and upset it often feels quite intense. In those situations, people have a tendency to over emphasize what caused the frustration. They tend to use words like *always* and *never*. Another common theme is to go into detail about what didn't work while completely leaving out the parts that did work. This can leave your partner feeling defeated; like nothing they do or say is right. It may cause them to ask, "Why would you still want to be in a relationship with someone who never does anything right?"

Look at the chart where your partner indicated their perceptions of how you experience their actions. Is it more closely aligned with what you observe or what you communicate? People need to feel appreciated. They want to know they have a positive impact on the relationship. They want to know that not only is the relationship important, but that it is worth the effort it takes to stay in it. There may be significant merit to the reason you are upset. However, when what you communicate does not line up with reality, both of you will feel stuck, hurt, and/or angry. This stalemate will continue until you are willing to acknowledge what your partner does do right.

No matter how frustrated you are, think about what your partner *does* do right. What do you appreciate about your partner? Choose the top 3 things that you appreciate and tell them. Look at the piece of the pie where you actually observed appreciating your partner and explain that piece to them. This will remind you of what is working and it will shift your partner from being defensive to actually being able to hear you.

Ask yourself what you are afraid of. All anger boils down to fear. If you are extremely angry, there is actually something you are tremendously afraid of. What is it? Take some time to really understand the fear. If you can't figure it out on your own, ask your partner for help. Maybe it is a blind spot for you. Maybe it is clear to your partner and you had no awareness of it at all. If not, maybe you can figure it out together.

When you can be honest and speak from the heart about what you appreciate as well as your fears, it creates a safe space for you both to be able to speak from your truth. It is in this place that you can have a healthy dialogue about what is and is not working. This is where the healing begins. This is how you can get to the other side where you actually feel closer to your partner than before the issue arose.

Understate

When you observe more frustration than you communicate (the observed % of frustration is more than the communicated % of frustration), it understates the extent to which you are actually upset with your partner. This can be much more subtle than overt anger; however no matter how much you try to hide it, there is still an impact. Your words and actions are not lining up. Your partner will either notice this or not.

If they don't notice, it is because you did not effectively communicate your true thoughts and feelings. Some people will cruise on believing everything is perfectly fine until you point out the contrary. There are people who would never notice there was a problem on their own. Your partner will never even attempt to make a change without first being aware of the issue. If they don't know about it, they can't fix it.

If your partner does notice that your words and your actions are not lining up, it will cause great anxiety for your partner that will take the form of confusion. You "say" you're okay, but your partner feels disconnected from you. They know something is wrong, but don't understand why.

When people downplay what they feel, they usually don't want to complain, say it will work itself out eventually, or believe there's no point in causing a scene because it wouldn't matter anyway. However, by remaining silent or only speaking part of your truth, you rob the relationship of the opportunity to heal. It is only through open and honest dialogue that the relationship can move past these issues that come up.

You have to find your voice. Talk to your partner about how you feel. Explain that you are afraid to be vulnerable. Tell them how difficult it is to say it at all. Say what is on your mind and in your heart. Speak your truth. The health of the relationship depends on it. When you can be courageous, it shifts the relationship from something you have to merely survive to a place where anything is possible. *This is where extraordinary relationships are created without guilt, shame, or fear.*

Positive Perspective

> *"The key to fanning the flame of hope is becoming intimate with your own positive perspective.
> It is through the lens of your positive perspective that you will begin to see the relationship in a different way."*

One of the most important attributes of a healthy relationship is that of *hope*. We trudge through the turmoil when it shows up because we believe that at the end of the day, it will be worth it. In the middle of the muck, there is a part of us that still clings to the notion that if we just hang in there everything will be okay. It is when hope is gone that we lose the will to continue. The warrior within us dissipates and we succumb to the idea that all is lost. Without hope, the relationship cannot recover.

The good news is that as long as there is a glimmer of a spark of hope there is enough light left to shine the way towards what we really want – an extraordinary relationship without guilt, shame, or fear. *The key to fanning the flame of hope is becoming intimate with your own positive perspective. It is through the lens of your positive perspective that you will begin to see the relationship in a different way.* It will remind you of why you wanted to get into this relationship in the first place. It will reconnect you with those feelings that drew you close to each other in the very beginning.

Try this exercise:

1. List your self-limiting beliefs in a column.
2. Replace the verbiage with a positive perspective.
3. In the next column indicate how you feel inside the positive perspective.
4. In the last column explain what it looks like inside the positive perspective.

Self-Limiting Belief	*Replace* it with a **Positive Perspective**	How do you **feel** inside the positive perspective?	What does it **look** like inside the positive perspective?

Source: (TS Production LLC, 2006)

Ask yourself what beliefs do you have about yourself that constrain you? What beliefs do you have that keep you from being your whole extraordinary self? What limitations do you put on yourself? Perhaps someone else gave you a label that was less than desirable and you took it on as though it were the truth. Regardless of whether or not you have evidence to substantiate a label, if it involves you feeling "less than" then it is a self-limiting belief. Write that down.

Now, examine that self-limiting belief and find a positive way to look at it. Pretend your task is that of a public relations expert who must "spin" a situation in a positive light. Ask yourself, "How can I turn this around to be something positive?" Rephrase the belief in such a way that it is something you would want to attach yourself to. Make it something worthy of you; something to be proud of. Write that down.

Next, think about this new positive perspective and imagine yourself inside it. Try it on like it was a new coat. Move around in it. Close your eyes and imagine being inside the positive perspective. How does it feel? What sensations do you feel inside your body? Write that down.

Once you have connected with the feeling of your positive perspective, close your eyes again and imagine what is around you. Visualize your surroundings. What do you see in your environment? Think of as much detail as you can. Imagine yourself there. What does your positive perspective look like inside that place? Write that down.

When you can connect with something that brings you joy, it places you in harmony with your extraordinary self. Now that you can verbalize, feel, and see a positive perspective, you no longer need the self-limiting belief. So... remove that column altogether. Get rid of it. It does not serve you. Throw away the self-limiting belief and focus on the positive perspective. Say it out loud. Close your eyes and feel the sensations in your body. See yourself within it. Imagine your surroundings. This is how you will shift your thought patterns from ones that detract to ones that will impact your life in a profound way.

The more honest you can be with yourself while going through this exercise, the more impact it will have on your viewpoint. If you can be courageous and choose a self-limiting belief that has a lot of emotional charge associated with it and truly examine it, you have the potential to create dramatic change. Be honest. You are worth the effort.

Now, go back and do this exercise from the perspective of the *relationship*. What limiting beliefs do you have about your partner? What limiting beliefs do you have about the relationship?* Then reframe them, connect with the joy, and see what happens. You may just find yourself in an *extraordinary relationship*.

***Author's Note**: *Notice if it is easier for you to be nonjudgmental about yourself or other people. Explore that dynamic.*

Judge-Your-Neighbor Worksheet

Judge your neighbor – Write it down – Ask four questions – Turn it around

Think of a recurring stressful situation that is reliably stressful even though it may have happened only once and recurs only in your mind. Before answering each of the questions below, allow yourself to mentally revisit the time and place of the stressful occurrence.

1. In this situation, time, and location, who angers, confuses, or disappoints you, and why?

    For example: *I am angry with Paul because he doesn't listen to me about his health.*

I am _____ with _____
                 (Emotion)   (Name)
because

_____

_____

_____

_____

2. In this situation, how do you want them to change? What do you want them to do?

   For example: *I want Paul to see that he is wrong. I want him to stop smoking. I want him to stop lying about what he is doing to his health. I want him to see that he is killing himself.*

   I want _____ to _____
                   (Name)

   _____

   _____

   _____

   _____

3. In this situation, what advice would you offer to them?

   For example: *Paul should take a deep breath. He should calm down. He should see that his actions scare me and the children. He should know that being right is not worth another heart attack.*

   _____   should/shouldn't
        (Name)

   _____

   _____

   _____

   _____

   _____

4. In order for *you* to be happy in this situation, what do you need them to think, say, feel, or do?

   For example: *I need Paul to hear me. I need him to take responsibility for his health. I need him to respect my opinions.*

   I need _____ to _____
                  (Name)

   _____

   _____

   _____

   _____

   _____

5. What do you think of them in that situation? Make a list.

   For example: *Paul is unfair, arrogant, loud, dishonest, way out of line, and unconscious.*

   _____ is _____
       (Name)

   _____

   _____

   _____

   _____

   _____

6. What is it in or about this situation that you don't ever want to experience again?

   For example: *I don't ever want Paul to lie to me again. I don't ever want to see him smoking and ruining his health again.*

   I don't ever want

   _____

   _____

   _____

   _____

   _____

   _____

Do you really want to know the truth? Investigate each of your statements using the four questions and the turnaround below. Leave out any statement beginning with "but," "because," or "and". Take only one negative judgment at a time through the process of inquiry. Often you will have several negative judgments about one person. Take each judgment separately through the inquiry process. The Work is a meditation. It's about awareness; it's not about trying to change your mind. Let the mind ask the questions, then contemplate. Take your time, go inside, and wait for the deeper answers to surface (Katie, 2011).

The Four Questions

For example: *Paul doesn't listen to me about his health.*

a) Is it true? *(Yes or no. If "no," move to 3).*
b) Can you absolutely know that it's true? *(Yes or no)*
c) How do you react, what happens, when you believe that thought?
d) Who would you be without that thought?

Here is an expansion of how the four questions apply to the statement *"Paul should understand me."*

1. **Is it true?** Is it true that he should understand you? Be still. Wait for the heart's response.

2. **Can you absolutely know that it's true?** Ultimately, can you really know what he should or shouldn't understand? Can you absolutely know what is in his best interest to understand?

3. **How do you react, what happens, when you believe that thought?** What happens when you believe "Paul should understand me" and he doesn't? Do you experience anger, stress, frustration? How do you treat Paul? Do you give him "the look"? Do you try to change him in any way? How do these reactions feel? How do you treat yourself? Does that thought bring stress or peace into your life? Be still as you listen.

4. **Who would you be without the thought?** Close your eyes. Picture yourself in the presence of Paul. Now imagine looking at Paul, just for a moment, without the thought "I want him to understand." What do you see? What would your life look like without that thought?

Use the following four questions and optional sub-questions with the concept that you are investigating. When answering the questions, close your eyes, be still, and go deeply as you contemplate. Inquiry stops working the moment you stop answering the questions (Katie, 2012, April).

Excerpt: (Katie, 2002, pp.247-250)

1. Is it true?

If your answer is "No" continue to question 3.

Possible follow-ups: (Katie, 2002)

- What is the reality of it?

- Did it happen? (This is often the first question to ask when the thought you're investigating involves a *should* --- "My husband should listen to me," "This shouldn't be happening." Inquiry is concerned only with reality. "He should" --- when he doesn't --- is a thought that argues with reality. This is not helpful when you're inquiring into what's true. What husbands should do is what they do. So the answer to, "He should care --- is it true?" will always be "No," until you think he does care. "This shouldn't be happening," couldn't possibly be true unless it isn't happening.)

2. Can you absolutely know that it's true?

Possible follow-ups: (Katie, 2002)

- Can you know more than God/reality?
- Whose business are you in?
- Can you really know what is best in the long run for his/her/your path?
- Can you absolutely know that you would be happier, or that your life would be better, if you got what you wanted?

3. How do you react when you believe that thought?

Possible follow-ups: (Katie, 2012, April)

- Does that thought bring peace or stress to your life?
- What physical sensations or emotions arise when you believe that thought? Allow yourself to experience them now.
- What images do you see, or past and future, when you believe that thought?
- What obsessions or addictions begin to manifest themselves when you are witnessing the images and believing the thought? (Do you act out on any of the following: alcohol, drugs, credit cards, food, sex, television, etc?)
- How do you treat that person, yourself, and others when you believe that thought?

4. Who would you be without the thought?

Close your eyes and observe, contemplate. Who or what are you without that thought? (Katie, 2012, April)

Possible follow-ups: (Katie, 2002)

- Who would you be if you didn't believe that thought?
- Close your eyes and imagine yourself with that person (or in that situation) without that thought. Describe how it feels. What do you see?
- Imagine that you are meeting this person for the very first time with no beliefs about him or her. What do you see?
- Who are you *right now*, sitting here without that thought?
- How would you live your life without that thought? If you were incapable of thinking that thought, how would your life be different?
- How would you treat others differently without that thought?

Turn the thought around

Next, turn your statement around. The turnarounds are an opportunity to experience the opposite of what you believe to be true. You may find several turnarounds (Katie, 2011).

For example, *"Paul should understand me"* turns around to:

- *I* should understand me.
- *I* should understand *Paul*.
- Paul *shouldn't* understand me.

Let yourself fully experience the turnarounds. For each one, find at least three genuine, specific examples in your life where the turnaround is true. This is not about blaming yourself or feeling guilty. It's about discovering alternatives that can bring you peace.

a) to the self. *(I don't listen to myself about my health.)*
b) to the other. *(I don't listen to Paul about his health.)*
c) to the opposite. *(Paul does listen to me about his health.)*

Excerpt: (Katie, 2002, pp.250, 253)

Statements can be turned around to yourself, to the other, and to the opposite. Find three examples in your life of where the turnarounds are as true or truer. Be specific and as detailed as you can.

Possible follow-ups:

- Is this turnaround as true as or truer than your original statement?
- Where do you experience this turnaround in your life now?
- If you lived this turnaround, what would you do, or how would you live differently?
- Do you see any other turnarounds that seem as true or truer?

The Turnaround for Number 6

The turnaround for statement number 6 is a little different:

"*I don't ever want to experience an argument with Paul again*" turns around to:

- "*I am willing to experience an argument with Paul again*," and
- "*I look forward to experiencing an argument with Paul again.*"

Number 6 is about welcoming all your thoughts and experiences with open arms, as it shows you where you are still at war with reality. If you feel any resistance to a thought, your Work is not done. When you can honestly look forward to experiences that have been uncomfortable, there is no longer anything to fear in life: you see everything as a gift that can bring you self-realization (Katie, 2011).

I am willing to _____

_____
_____
_____
_____
_____

I am willing to have Paul lie to me again.

I look forward to _____

_____
_____
_____
_____
_____

For example: *I look forward to having Paul lie to me again.*

Sample Judge-Your-Neighbor Worksheet Completed

Judge-Your-Neighbor Worksheet

Judge your neighbor – Write it down – Ask four questions – Turn it around

Think of a recurring stressful situation that is reliably stressful even though it may have happened only once and recurs only in your mind. Before answering each of the questions below, allow yourself to mentally revisit the time and place of the stressful occurrence.

1. In this situation, time, and location, who angers, confuses, or disappoints you, and why?

   I am angry with John because he does not make the relationship a priority.

2. In this situation, how do you want them to change? What do you want them to do?

   I want John to be in a committed relationship with me. I want him to want to stay with me after his trip is over. I want him to acknowledge when he's wrong instead of me always being the one to admit fault.

3. In this situation, what advice would you offer to them?

John should consider my feelings when he makes significant decisions that impact the relationship. He should ask what I want instead of only announcing what he wants. He should stop being so afraid and believe that I won't hurt him.

4. In order for you to be happy in this situation, what do you need them to think, say, feel, or do?

I need John to dialogue with me before making big decisions that affect us. I need him to tell his friends and family about me. I need him to include me in his future. I want him to believe in me and see what's possible instead of being hyper critical.

5. What do you think of them in that situation? Make a list.

John is selfish, arrogant, hyper critical, and oblivious.

6. What is it in or about this situation that you don't ever want to experience again?

I don't ever want to let John down or disappoint him to the extent that he stops loving me and leaves me.

The Four Questions

John does not make the relationship a priority.

a) Is it true?

No

b) Can you absolutely know that it's true?

n/a

c) How do you react, what happens, when you believe that thought?

I become afraid that he doesn't love me, he doesn't like me anymore, and that he is going to leave.

d) Who would you be without that thought?

I would trust that he loves me and that he has no intention of going anywhere. I would feel calm, centered, and balanced.

Turn the thought around

John does not make the relationship a priority.

a) to the self.

I don't make the relationship a priority when I get stuck in my fear. I make things worse by giving in to old patterns and letting fear consume me.

b) to the other.

I don't listen when John tells me the relationship is a priority. He told me he loved me and I was afraid it was a fear-based announcement because he said it for the first time when I was upset. He has said it since then without provocation and in the moment when it was meaningful. John does love me.

c) to the opposite.

John does make the relationship a priority. He drives the 3 ½ hours here every chance he is free. He spends all of his free time with me. He chooses to be with me when he could be anywhere else.

The turnaround for statement 6.

I don't ever want to let John down or disappointment him to the extent that he stops loving me and leaves me.

I am willing to let John stop loving me and leave me if it means he can be happy.

I look forward to letting John stop loving me and leave me if it means he can be happy.

Nonviolent Communication Model

Fill out the worksheet based on your experience (Part 1) and what you believe to be your partner's experience (Part 2). Then have a dialogue with your partner about what you filled out (Part 3).

Part 1: Honestly Expressing

> **Observation**: "When…"
> *(something you can observe: see or hear)*
>
> **Feeling**: "I feel…"
> *(inner emotions and bodily sensations)*
>
> **Need**: "Because I need…"
> *(needs and values)*
>
> **Request**: "Would you be willing to…"
> *(specific desired behavior that can be observed; include time/day, etc)*

Part 2: Empathetically Listening

> **Observation**: "When…"
>
> **Feeling**: "Do you feel…?"
>
> **Need**: "Because you need…"
>
> **Request**: "Would you like…?"

Adapted with permission: © 2006 by Center for Nonviolent Communication, www.cnvc.org, cnvc@cnvc.org, (505) 244-4041

Sample NVC Model Worksheet Completed

Part 1: Honestly Expressing

Observation: When you yell at me

Feeling:

> (*emotions*): I feel scared, hurt, and sad

> (*bodily sensations*): I feel my breathing stop, I hold my breath, my chest tightens, numbness comes into my stomach and flows upwards out to my arms and up through my face

Need: because I need to feel connected and safe.

Request: Would you be willing to slow down, hold my hands, calmly express your needs and reassure me you still love me, can imagine not being angry anymore, and still want to be in relationship with me?

Part 2: Empathetically Listening

Observation: When you yell at me

Feeling:

    (*emotions*): do you feel annoyed, angry and baffled?

    (*bodily sensations*):

Need: because you need safety (order, security, and stability)?

Request: Would you like me to slow down, get out of my head, and pay attention to what we are doing in the moment?

Part 3: Discussion

After the above points are discussed, since the observation involves anger and because all anger boils down to fear, then ask:

    What are you afraid of?

When I Say...

Often times what we say and what we mean are two completely different things. Sit with your partner, hold each other's hands, look into their eyes, and explore, "When I say _____, what I *really* mean is _____" (Torma, 2012).

<u>Examples</u>

"When I say I don't want to be in relationship with you any more, what I *really* mean is I need to connect with you in that moment more than ever."

"When I say I can handle everything, what I *really* mean is I need your help. I'm just afraid to ask for it."

"When I say I'm independent and don't need your help, what I *really* mean is I want for you to take care of me. I just don't know how to receive."

"When I say I'm brave and nothing gets to me, what I *really* mean is I am afraid because I don't know how to be vulnerable."

"When I say it is okay when you're feeling weak because I will take care of you, what I *really* mean is I want for you to take care of me sometimes. I want for you to be the strong one every now and then."

"When I say I'm angry, what I *really* mean is I am so afraid that I just don't know what to do."

60-Day Fear Challenge

Working with the underlying fear is one of the highest leverage aspects of the framework. If you threw out all of the other concepts presented in the framework and merely kept this one little piece and worked on it, your relationship would be unrecognizable in two-months.

Make a commitment to each other that over the next 60-days each time anger appears, stop and purposefully examine the underlying fears. Ask questions like:

- What am I really afraid of?
- If I'm mad about _____, then what is the fear underneath?
- What scares me about this situation?

Take the time to make a mental inventory of the state of the relationship as it is today. Purposefully create a dialogue each and every time anger appears. Don't wait until the upset has festered. Stop and take care of it right away. Do it right then.

Be kind to each other as you go through this process. Shining the light on your deepest fears can be a scary proposition. Your lizard brain will try its best to protect you and distract you from this activity. Stick with it. This is *important*. It can have such an enormous impact on the state of the relationship and on you as an individual. There is opportunity for *real* growth inside this space.

After 60-days, check in again and take another mental inventory of the state of the relationship. It may just be completely unrecognizable – and *extraordinary*.

About the Author

Alexis C. Bell lives in Charlotte, North Carolina, USA with her youngest daughter. Her eldest daughter, son-in-law, and grandchildren live nearby.

Alexis is a professional woman with global responsibilities. She was able to overcome many obstacles during her professional career to achieve a level of success that was quite far away from her starting point. Those situations spilled over into her personal life and allowed her the opportunity to gain a measure of expertise in relationships. She was able to analyze the underlying reasons the relationship either failed or became successful. She wanted to use her experiences along with the stories of those close to her as the foundation to communicate the message. The resulting framework became the structure for this book where she is able to share the lessons which made a difference in her life and for those around her.

References

Berens, L. V. (1998). *Understanding Yourself and Others: An Introduction to Temperament*. Huntington Beach, CA: Telos Publications.

Chapman, G. (1992/2010). *The 5 Love Languages: The Secret to Love That Lasts*. Chicago, IL: Northfield Publishing. www.5LoveLanguages.com

Clearing Energy Work. (2012). Charlotte, NC. http://www.ClearingEnergyWork.com

Cliffs Notes. (n.d.) Hoboken, NJ: John Wiley & Sons, Inc. http://www.cliffsnotes.com

Covey, S. R. (2000). *The 7 Habits of Highly Effective People*. Philadelphia, PA: Running Press.

Dagley, J. (1978, April 8). Deaf-Blind Woman's Mind Unlimited: The story of Tommie Goins. *NAT-CENT News*, (pp. 9-13).

d'Ansembourg, T. (n.d.). Nonviolent Communication: List of NON-Feeling Words and Thoughts. *Being Genuine* [supplement]. Puddle Dancer Press. www.nonviolentcommunication.com

Epstein, D. (n.d.). Network Spinal Analysis. http://www.donaldepstein.com

Godin, S. (n.d.). *Quieting the Lizard Brain* [video]. Insights on Making Ideas Happen. Behance, Inc. Retrieved from, http://the99percent.com/videos/5822/Seth-Godin-Quieting-the-Lizard-Brain

Harris, P. (Producer & Director). (2004). *Crash*. United States. Lionsgate.

Hohl, D., & Karinch, M. (2003). *Rangers Lead the Way: The Army Rangers' Guide to Leading Your Organization Through Chaos.* Avon, MA: Adams Media Corporation.

Howard, P. (2006). *The Owner's Manual for the Brain: Everyday Applications from Mind-Brain Research* (3rd Edition). Austin, TX: Bard Press.

Katie, B. (2002). *I Need Your Love – Is That True?* New York, NY: Three Rivers Press.

Katie, B. (2011, January 21). *Instructions for Doing the Work.* The Work of Byron Katie. Byron Katie International, Inc. Retrieved from, http://www.thework.com/downloads/worksheets/instructions_for_thework.pdf

Katie, B. (2012, April 27). *Facilitation Guide: For the Work of Byron Katie, Four Questions & Turnaround.* Byron Katie International, Inc. Retrieved from, http://www.thework.com/downloads/worksheets/facilitationguide_Eng.pdf

Katie, B. (2012, May 30). *Judge-Your-Neighbor Worksheet.* The Work of Byron Katie. Byron Katie International, Inc. Retrieved from, http://www.thework.com/downloads/worksheets/JudgeYourNeighbor_Worksheet.pdf

Keirsey, D. (1998, May). *Please Understand Me II: Temperament, Character, Intelligence.* Del Mar, CA: Prometheus Nemesis Book Company.

Knight, S. (2002). *NLP at Work: The difference that makes a difference in business* (Second Edition). London, United Kingdom: Nicholas Brealey Publishing.

Lasater, I. (2003). Evaluations Masquerading As Feelings. *Words That Work.* Warsaw, Poland. http://wordsthatwork.us/site/

Margulies, S. & Wolper, D. L. (Producer), & Stuart, M. (Director). (1971). *Willy Wonka & the Chocolate Factory*. United States: Warner Brothers.

Maslow, A. (1954 / 1987). *Motivation and Personality*. New York, NY: Harper & Row Publishers, Inc.

Max-Neef, M. (1992). Development and Human Needs. In Ekins, P., Max-Neef, M. (Eds.), *Real-Life Economics: Understanding Wealth Creation,* pp. 197-213. Routledge, London.

Myers, I. B. (1998). *Introduction to Type* (6th Ed.). Palo Alto, CA: Consulting Psychologists Press, Inc.

Myers & Briggs Foundation. (2003). *Myers-Briggs Type Indicator (MBTI)*. Retrieved July 20, 2012 from, www.myersbriggs.org

Ortho-Bionomy. (n.d.). Society of Ortho-Bionomy International. http://www.ortho-bionomy.org

Rosenberg, M. (2010, October 26). *Nonviolent Communication (NVC) Model*. Albuquerque, NM: The Center for Nonviolent Communication. https://www.cnvc.org/Training/the-nvc-model

Rosenberg, M. (2006, November 9). *Feelings Inventory*. Albuquerque, NM: The Center for Nonviolent Communication. http://www.cnvc.org/Training/feelings-inventory

Torma, S. (2012, June 21-24). *The Art of Intimacy: Compassionate Communication in Relationships and Friendships, Levels 1 and 2* at the Firefly Gathering in Hendersonville, NC [symposium]. Asheville, NC: The REAL Center. http://www.theREALcenter.org

TS Production LLC (Producer), & Hariot, D. (Director). (2006). *The Secret* [Extended Edition, DVD]. Available from www.TheSecret.tv

Williamson, M. (1992). *A Return to Love: Reflections on the Principles of "A Course in Miracles."* New York, NY: HarperCollins Publishers.

Appendix A – Myers-Briggs® Personality Types

ISTJ	ISFJ	INFJ	INTJ
ISTP	ISFP	INFP	INTP
ESTP	ESFP	ENFP	ENTP
ESTJ	ESFJ	ENFJ	ENTJ

ISTJ	Quiet, serious, earn success by thoroughness and dependability. Practical, matter-of-fact, realistic, and responsible. Decide logically what should be done and work toward it steadily, regardless of distractions. Take pleasure in making everything orderly and organized – their work, their home, their life. Value traditions and loyalty.
ISTP	Tolerant and flexible, quiet observers until a problem appears, then act quickly to find workable solutions. Analyze what makes things work and readily get through large amounts of data to isolate the core of practical problems. Interested in cause and effect, organize facts using logical principles, value efficiency.
ESTP	Flexible and tolerant, they take a pragmatic approach focused on immediate results. Theories and conceptual explanations bore them – they want to act energetically to solve the problem. Focus on the here-and-now, spontaneous, enjoy each moment that they can be active with others. Enjoy material comforts and style. Learn best through doing.
ESTJ	Practical, realistic, matter-of-fact. Decisive, quickly move to implement decisions. Organize projects and people to get things done, focus on getting results in the most efficient way possible. Take care of routine details. Have a clear set of logical standards, systematically follow them and want others to also. Forceful in implementing their plans.

ISFJ	Quiet, friendly, responsible, and conscientious. Committed and steady in meeting their obligations. Thorough, painstaking, and accurate. Loyal, considerate, notice and remember specifics about people who are important to them, concerned with how others feel. Strive to create an orderly and harmonious environment at work and at home.
ISFP	Quiet, friendly, sensitive, and kind. Enjoy the present moment, what's going on around them. Like to have their own space and to work within their own time frame. Loyal and committed to their values and to people who are important to them. Dislike disagreements and conflicts, do not force their opinions or values on others.
ESFP	Outgoing, friendly, and accepting. Exuberant lovers of life, people, and material comforts. Enjoy working with others to make things happen. Bring common sense and a realistic approach to their work, and make work fun. Flexible and spontaneous, adapt readily to new people and environments. Learn best by trying a new skill with other people.
ESFJ	Warmhearted, conscientious, and cooperative. Want harmony in their environment, work with determination to establish it. Like to work with others to complete tasks accurately and on time. Loyal, follow through even in small matters. Notice what others need in their day-by-day lives and try to provide it. Want to be appreciated for who they are and for what they contribute.
INFJ	Seek meaning and connection in ideas, relationships, and material possessions. Want to understand what motivates people and are insightful about others. Conscientious and committed to their firm values. Develop a clear vision about how best to serve the common good. Organized and decisive in implementing their vision.

INFP	Idealistic, loyal to their values and to people who are important to them. Want an external life that is congruent with their values. Curious, quick to see possibilities, can be catalysts for implementing ideas. Seek to understand people and to help them fulfill their potential. Adaptable, flexible, and accepting unless a value is threatened.
ENFP	Warmly enthusiastic and imaginative. See life as full of possibilities. Make connections between events and information very quickly, and confidently proceed based on the patterns they see. Want a lot of affirmation from others, and readily give appreciation and support. Spontaneous and flexible, often rely on their ability to improvise and their verbal fluency.
ENFJ	Warm, empathetic, responsive, and responsible. Highly attuned to the emotions, needs, and motivations of others. Find potential in everyone, want to help others fulfill their potential. May act as catalysts for individual and group growth. Loyal, responsive to praise and criticism. Sociable, facilitate others in a group, and provide inspiring leadership.
INTJ	Have original minds and great drive for implementing their ideas and achieving their goals. Quickly see patterns in external events and develop long-range explanatory perspectives. When committed, organize a job and carry it through. Skeptical and independent, have high standards of competence and performance – for themselves and others.
INTP	Seek to develop logical explanations for everything that interests them. Theoretical and abstract, interested more in ideas than in social interaction. Quiet, contained, flexible, and adaptable. Have unusual ability to focus in depth to solve problems in their area of interest. Skeptical, sometimes critical, always analytical.

ENTP	Quick, ingenious, stimulating, alert, and outspoken. Resourceful in solving new and challenging problems. Adept at generating conceptual possibilities and then analyzing them strategically. Good at reading other people. Bored by routine, will seldom do the same thing the same way, apt to turn to one new interest after another.
ENTJ	Frank, decisive, assume leadership readily. Quickly see illogical and inefficient procedures and policies, develop and implement comprehensive systems to solve organizational problems. Enjoy long-term planning and goal setting. Usually well informed, well read, enjoy expanding their knowledge and passing it on to others. Forceful in presenting their ideas.

© Myers-Briggs®, Myers-Briggs Type Indicator®, MBTI®, and Personality Differences Questionnaire® are all registered trademarks with CPP, Inc. Modified and reproduced by special permission of the Publisher, CPP, Inc. Mountain View, CA 94043 from Introduction to Type, Sixth Edition by Isabel Briggs Myers. Copyright 1998 by Peter B. Myers and Katharine D. Myers. All rights reserved. Further reproduction is prohibited without the Publisher's written consent.

Appendix B – Sex & Gender Differences in the Brain

The following table details the differences in the brain by sex and gender.

© 2006 Pierce J. Howard, PhD, *The Owner's Manual for the Brain: Everyday Applications From Mind-Brain Research*, Appendix B – Sex and Gender Differences, pp. 906-907.

As cited from the original source of: Based on Anne Moir and David Jessel (1991), *Brain Sex: The Real Difference Between Men and Women*. New York, NY: Carol Publishing/Lyle Stuart.

Males	**Females**
Have better general math ability	Have better general verbal ability
Are better at spatial (3-D) reasoning	Are better in grammar and vocabulary
Are better at chess	Are better at foreign languages
Are better at reading maps	Have better fine motor (hand-eye) coordination within personal space
Are better at reading blueprints	
Have better vision in bright lights (see less well in darkness)	Have better sensory awareness
Have better perception in blue end of spectrum	Have better night vision (are more sensitive to bright light)
Have more narrow vision (tunnel vision), but depth and perspective	Have better perception in red end of spectrum
Have more stuttering and speech defects	Have wide peripheral vision for "big picture"; have more receptor rods and cones
Enroll more in remedial reading (4:1)	Perceive sounds better
Take more interest in objects	Sing in tune more (6:1)
Talk and play more with inanimate objects	Are more interested in people and faces
	Read character and social cues better

Males

Preschoolers:

- Average 36 seconds for goodbyes
- Occupy more play space
- Prefer blocks and building
- Build high structures
- Are indifferent to newcomers
- Accept others if they are useful
- Prefer stories of adventure
- Identify more with robbers
- Play more competitive games such as tag
- Use dolls for "dive bombers"
- Are better visual-spatial learners

Require more space

Have a better aural memory

Are more easily angered

Talk later (usually by 4- years of age)

Are more sensitive to and prefer salty tastes

Have relatively insensitive skin

Have right hemisphere larger than left

Favor right ear

Females

Preschoolers:

- Average 93 seconds for goodbyes
- Occupy less play space
- Prefer playing with living things
- Build long and low structures
- Greet newcomers
- Accept others if they are nice
- Prefer stories of romance
- Identify more with victims
- Play less competitive games, e.g. hopscotch
- Use dolls for family scenes
- Are better auditory learners

Require less space

Have a better visual memory

Are slower to anger

Talk earlier (99% are understandable by 3-years of age)

Are more sensitive to bitter tastes; prefer sweets and more subtle tastes

Have extremely sensitive skin

Have left hemisphere larger than right

Listen equally with both ears

Males	**Females**
Solve math problems nonverbally	Tend to talk while solving math problems
Handle multitasking more easily	Are less at ease with multitasking
Have better memory for relevant or organized information	Have better memory for names and faces and for random and irrelevant information
Use less eye contact	Use more eye contact
Have a shorter attention span	Have a longer attention span
Don't notice the smell of Exaltolide (a musklike odor)	Are especially sensitive to the smell of Exaltolide, especially before ovulation
Are more sensation-seeking	Are less sensation-seeking (but American females are more sensation-seeking than English females)
Are more frequently left-handed than females	Are more frequently right-handed than males
Use left hemisphere in spelling	Use both hemispheres in spelling
Have differentiated hemispheres; right for math and spatial skills and left for language	Have undifferentiated hemispheres
Have corpus callosum that shrinks about 20% by the age of 50 and is thinner relative to brain size	Have corpus callosum that is thicker relative to brain size and doesn't shrink over time
Have left hemisphere that shrinks with age	Have left hemisphere that shrinks systematically and minimally

Males	**Females**
Prefer greater distance from same-sex others	Are more comfortable than men are when they are physically close to same-sex others
Are three times more likely to be dyslexic or myopic	Are less likely to be dyslexic or myopic
React to pain slowly	React to pain more quickly; can tolerate long-term pain or discomfort better
Report feeling less pain	Report feeling more pain
Cope with pain less well	Cope with pain better
When left alone, tend to form organizations with hierarchical, dominant structures	When left alone, tend to form informal organizations with shifting power sources
Interrupt to introduce new topics or information	Interrupt to clarify or support

Appendix C –
Feelings when your needs are NOT satisfied

AFRAID
apprehensive
dread
foreboding
frightened
mistrustful
panicked
petrified
scared
suspicious
terrified
wary
worried

ANNOYED
aggravated
dismayed
disgruntled
displeased
exasperated
frustrated
impatient
irritated
irked

ANGRY
enraged
furious
incensed
indignant
irate
livid
outraged
resentful

AVERSION
animosity
appalled
contempt
disgusted
dislike
hate
horrified
hostile
repulsed

CONFUSED
ambivalent
baffled
bewildered
dazed
hesitant
lost
mystified
perplexed
puzzled
torn

DISCONNECTED
alienated
aloof
apathetic
bored
cold
detached
distant
miserable
regretful

distracted
indifferent
numb
removed
uninterested
withdrawn

DISQUIET
agitated
alarmed
discombobulated
disconcerted
disturbed
perturbed
rattled
restless
shocked
startled
surprised
troubled
turbulent
turmoil
uncomfortable
uneasy
unnerved
unsettled
upset

EMBARRASSED
ashamed
chagrined
flustered
guilty
mortified
self-conscious

FATIGUE
beat
burnt out
depleted
exhausted
lethargic
listless
sleepy
tired
weary
worn out

PAIN
agony
anguished
bereaved
devastated
grief
heartbroken
hurt
lonely
remorseful

SAD
depressed
dejected
despair
despondent
disappointed
discouraged
disheartened
forlorn
gloomy
heavy hearted
hopeless
melancholy
unhappy
wretched

TENSE
anxious
cranky
distressed
distraught
edgy
fidgety
frazzled
irritable
jittery
nervous
overwhelmed
restless
stressed out

VULNERABLE
fragile
guarded
helpless
insecure
leery
reserved
sensitive
shaky

YEARNING
envious
jealous
longing
nostalgic
pining
wistful

Reprinted with permission: © 2006 by Center for Nonviolent Communication, www.cnvc.org, cnvc@cnvc.org, (505) 244-4041

Appendix D – Feelings when your needs ARE satisfied

AFFECTIONATE
compassionate
friendly
loving
open hearted
sympathetic
tender
warm

ENGAGED
absorbed
alert
curious
engrossed
enchanted
entranced
fascinated
interested
intrigued
involved
spellbound
stimulated

HOPEFUL
expectant
encouraged
optimistic

CONFIDENT
empowered
open
proud
safe
secure

EXCITED
amazed
animated
ardent
aroused
astonished
dazzled
eager
energetic
enthusiastic
giddy
invigorated
lively
passionate
surprised
vibrant

GRATEFUL
appreciative
moved
thankful
touched

INSPIRED
amazed
awed
wonder

JOYFUL
amused
delighted
glad
happy
jubilant
pleased
tickled

EXHILARATED
blissful
ecstatic
elated
enthralled
exuberant
radiant
rapturous
thrilled

PEACEFUL
calm
clear headed
comfortable
centered
content
equanimous
fulfilled
mellow
quiet
relaxed
relieved
satisfied
serene
still
tranquil
trusting

REFRESHED
enlivened
rejuvenated
renewed
rested
restored
revived

Reprinted with permission: © 2006 by Center for Nonviolent Communication, www.cnvc.org, cnvc@cnvc.org, (505) 244-4041

Appendix E –
Evaluations Masquerading As Feelings

For example, when I say, "I feel criticized by you." I am probably telling you my interpretation of your conduct. And further I am probably suggesting you are doing something to me with a connotation of wrongness or blame. Instead, I would prefer to focus on which of my needs I am concerned with not being met by what you said or did and how I am feeling as a result. The following might be suggestions intended as an aid to get to the feeling and needs that are behind these kinds of evaluation words.

When You SAY:	What Might You Be FEELING?	What Might You Be NEEDING?
Abandoned	Terrified, hurt, bewildered, sad, frightened, lonely	Nurturing, connection, belonging, support, caring
Abused	Angry, frustrated, frightened	Caring, nurturing, support, emotional or physical wellbeing, consideration, need for all living things to flourish
Attacked	Scared, angry	Safety

When You SAY:	What Might You Be FEELING?	What Might You Be NEEDING?
Belittled	Angry, frustrated, tense, distressed	Respect, autonomy, to be seen, acknowledgment, appreciation
Betrayed	Angry, hurt, disappointed, enraged	Trust, dependability, honesty, honor, commitment, clarity
Blamed	Angry, scared, confused, antagonistic, hostile, bewildered, hurt	Accountability, causality, fairness, justice
Cheated	Resentful, hurt, angry	Honesty, fairness, justice, trust, reliability
Coerced	Angry, frustrated, frightened, thwarted, scared	Choice, autonomy, freedom, act freely, choose freely
Cornered	Angry, scared, anxious, thwarted,	Autonomy, freedom

When You SAY:	What Might You Be FEELING?	What Might You Be NEEDING?
Criticized	In pain, scared, anxious, frustrated, humiliated, angry, embarrassed	Understanding, acknowledgement, recognition, accountability, non-judgmental communication
Harassed	Angry, frustrated, pressured, frightened	Respect, space, consideration, peace
Hassled	Irritated, distressed, angry, frustrated	Serenity, autonomy, do things at my own pace and in my own way, calm, space
Ignored	Lonely, scared, hurt, sad, embarrassed	Connection, belonging, inclusion, community, participation
Insulted	Angry, embarrassed	Respect, consideration, acknowledgment, recognition

When You SAY:	What Might You Be FEELING?	What Might You Be NEEDING?
Intimidated	Scared, anxiety	Safety, equality, empowerment
Invalidated	Angry, hurt, resentful	Appreciation, respect, acknowledgement, recognition
Invisible	Sad, angry, lonely, scared	To be seen and heard, inclusion, belonging, community
Isolated	Lonely, afraid, scared	Community, inclusion, belonging, ;contribution
Left out	Sad, lonely, anxious	Inclusion, belonging, community, connection
Let down	Sad, disappointed, frightened	Consistency, trust, dependability, consistency
Manipulated	Angry, scared, powerless, thwarted, frustrated	Autonomy, empowerment, trust, equality, freedom, free choice, connection, genuineness

When You SAY:	What Might You Be FEELING?	What Might You Be NEEDING?
Mistrusted	Sad, angry	Trust
Misunderstood	Upset, angry, frustrated	To be heard, understanding, clarity
Neglected	Lonely, scared	Connection, inclusion, participation, community, care, mattering, consideration
Patronized	Angry, frustrated, resentful	Recognition, equality, respect, mutuality
Pressured	Anxious, resentful, overwhelmed	Relaxation, clarity, space, consideration
Provoked	Angry, frustrated, hostile, antagonistic, resentful	Respect, consideration
Put down	Angry, sad, embarrassed	Respect, acknowledgment, understanding

When You SAY:	What Might You Be FEELING?	What Might You Be NEEDING?
Rejected	Hurt, scared, angry, defiant	Belonging, inclusion, closeness, to be seen, acknowledgment, connection
Ripped off/screwed	Angry, resentment, disappointment	Consideration, justice, fairness, acknowledgement, trust
Smothered/Suffocated	Frustrated, fear, desperation	Space, freedom, autonomy, authenticity, self-expression
Taken for granted	Sad, angry, hurt, disappointment	Appreciation, acknowledgment, recognition, consideration
Threatened	Scared, frightened, alarmed, agitated, defiant	Safety, autonomy
Unappreciated	Angry, hurt, frustrated	Appreciation, respect, acknowledgement, consideration
Unheard	Sad, hostile, frustrated	Understanding, consideration, empathy

When You SAY:	What Might You Be FEELING?	What Might You Be NEEDING?
Unloved	Sad, bewildered, frustrated	Love, appreciation, empathy, connection, community
Unseen	Sad, anxious, frustrated	Acknowledgment, appreciation, to be heard
Unsupported	Sad, hurt, resentful	Support, understanding
Unwanted	Sad, anxious, frustrated	Belonging, inclusion, caring
Used	Sad, angry, resentful	Autonomy, equality, consideration, mutuality
Victimized	Frightened, helpless	Empowerment, mutuality, safety, justice
Violated	Sad, agitated, anxiety	Privacy, safety, trust, space, respect
Wronged	Angry, hurt, resentful, irritated	Respect, justice, trust, safety, fairness

Reprinted with permission:
© 2003 Ike Lasater, Words That Work, http://www.wordsthatwork.us

Appendix F – Matrix of Needs and Satisfiers

Fundamental Human Needs [a]	Needs According to Existential [b] Categories			
	Being [c]	Having [d]	Doing [e]	Interacting [f]
Sustenance	Physical health, mental health, equilibrium, sense of humor, adaptability	Food, shelter, work	Feed, procreate, rest, work	Living environment, social setting

Note. The first column represents Needs According to Axiological Categories.
[a] Where *axiology* is the philosophical study of values (ethics and aesthetics) and value judgments; *Ethics* involves "right" and "wrong" of individuals and society; *Aesthetics* studies the nature of beauty, art, and taste.
[b] Where *existential* is a philosophical and cultural movement governed by authenticity; to be *authentic* means to be true to one's own self.
[c] Being: *Attributes*, personal or collective, that are expressed as nouns.
[d] Having: *Institutions, norms, mechanisms, tools, laws*, etc.
[e] Doing: *Actions*, personal or collective.
[f] Interacting: In the sense of time and space (English translation).

Source: Max-Neef (1992), Table 7.1 Matrix of Needs and Satisfiers.

Fundamental Human Needs	Needs According to Existential Categories			
	Being	Having	Doing	Interacting
Protection	Care, adaptability, autonomy, equilibrium, solidarity	Insurance systems, savings, social security, health systems, rights, family, work	Cooperate, prevent, plan, take care of, cure, help	Living space, social environment, dwelling
Affection	Self-esteem, solidarity, respect, tolerance, generosity, receptiveness, passion, determination, sensuality, sense of humor	Friendships, family, partnerships, relationships with nature	Make love, caress, express emotions, share, take care of, cultivate, appreciate	Privacy, intimacy, home, spaces of togetherness
Understanding	Critical conscience, receptiveness, curiosity, astonishment, discipline, intuition, rationality	Literature, teachers, method, educational policies, communication policies	Investigate, study, experiment, educate, analyze, meditate	Settings of formative interaction, schools, universities, academics, groups, communities, family

Fundamental Human Needs	Needs According to Existential Categories			
	Being	Having	Doing	Interacting
Participation	Adaptability, receptiveness, solidarity, willingness, determination, dedication, respect, passion, sense of humor	Rights, responsibilities, duties, privileges, work	Become affiliated, cooperate, propose, share, dissent, obey, interact, agree on, express opinions	Settings of participative interaction, parties, associations, churches, communities, neighborhoods, family
Leisure	Curiosity, receptiveness, imagination, recklessness, sense of humor, tranquility, sensuality	Games, spectacles, clubs, parties, peace of mind	Day-dream, brood, dream, recall old times, give away to fantasies, remember, relax, have fun, play	Privacy, intimacy, spaces of closeness, free time, surroundings, landscapes
Creation	Passion, determination, intuition, imagination, boldness, rationality, autonomy, inventiveness, curiosity	Abilities, skills, method, work	Work, invent, build, design, compose, interpret	Productive and feedback settings, workshops, cultural groups, audiences, spaces for expression, temporal freedom

Fundamental Human Needs	Needs According to Existential Categories			
	Being	Having	Doing	Interacting
Identity	Sense of belonging, consistency, differentiation, self-esteem, assertiveness	Symbols, language, religions, habits, customs, reference, groups, sexuality, values, norms, historical memory, work	Commit oneself, integrate oneself, confront, decide on, get to know oneself, recognize oneself, actualize oneself, grow	Social rhythms, everyday settings, settings which one belongs to, maturation stages
Freedom	Autonomy, self-esteem, determination, passion, assertiveness, open-mindedness, boldness, rebelliousness, tolerance	Equal rights	Dissent, choose, be, different from, run risks, develop awareness, commit oneself, disobey	Temporal / spatial plasticity

Appendix G – Needs Inventory

SUSTENANCE
air
balance
calm
exercise
flexibility
food
joy
mental health
nature
peace
physical health
rest
sexual expression
shelter
stability
touch
water
wellbeing
   (of someone else)
work

PROTECTION
care for
discipline
justice
mourning
order
safety
security

AFFECTION
acceptance
appreciation
companionship
connection
generosity
harmony
intimacy
love
nurturing
relationship
sensuality
warmth

UNDERSTANDING
authenticity
awareness
clarity
communication
compassion
empathy
heard (to be)
growth
intuition
open-mindedness
presence (be present)
tolerance
trust
wisdom

PARTICIPATION
belonging
community
cooperation
consideration
consistency
contribution
equality
fairness
inclusion
mutuality
support
willingness

LEISURE
adventure
beauty
humor
peace
play
relaxation
tranquility

CREATION
discovery
imagination
inspiration
passion
self-expression

IDENTITY
challenge
differentiation
empowerment
honesty
honor
integrity
independence
know (to know / be known)
respect (for self / others)
seen (to see / be seen)
self-esteem
values

FREEDOM
assertiveness
boldness
choice
rebelliousness
solitude
space
spontaneity

MEANING
awareness
celebration of life
challenge
clarity
competence
consciousness
contribution
creativity
discovery
efficacy
effectiveness
growth
hope
learning
mourning
participation
purpose
self-expression
stimulation
to matter
understanding

Adapted from the *Feelings Inventory* by Dr. Marshall B. Rosenberg.
© 2005 by Center for Nonviolent Communication
Website: www.cnvc.org Email: cnvc@cnvc.org Phone: +1.505.244.4041